Recipes from Nature

Foraging Through the Seasons

Kay and Bill Lindner

Creative Publishing international

Chanhassen, Minnesota

Kay Lindner writes feature stories and food columns for many prestigious outdoor magazines, including *The Florida Sportsman* and *Bass Pro Outdoor World*. Bill Lindner is a nationally known, professional outdoor and food photographer. His work has appeared in many books and magazines for more than 25 years. They live in Minneapolis, MN.

Creative Publishing
international

President/CEO: Ken Fund
Vice President/Publisher: Linda Ball
Vice President/Retail Sales & Marketing: Kevin Haas
Executive Editor, Outdoor Group: Barbara Harold
Creative Director: Brad Springer
Book Designer: Jeff Franke
Food Stylists: Betsy Nelson, Susan Telleen, Abby Wyckoff
Assistant Food Stylist: Maggie Stopera
Photo Assistant: Georgina Frankel
Prop Styling: Rhonda Watkins
Image Management: Mike Hehner
Project Management: Denise Bornhausen
Production: Lacey Criswell, Vanessa Leah
Metric Conversions: Ellen Boeke
Recipe Consultant: Rachel Rdybeck
Production Manager: Laura Hokkanen

Printed in China
10 9 8 7 6 5 4 3 2 1

Dedication

To our lovely newborn baby daughter, Valerie May,
a gift from God.

To my father, Robert Wethern, and to Bill's parents, Ron and
Dolores Lindner—for your love, prayers, and guidance.

Acknowledgments

Special thanks go to Denise Bornhausen, for your dedication,
stamina, and positive attitude during your project management
of this book; and to Mike Hehner, stock photo manager of
Bill Lindner Photography.

Our sincere gratitude goes to all the people who contributed
recipes. Thank you for sharing your love and passion for foods
from the outdoors!

Tim Anderson, Matt Annand, Don Berger, Susan Binkley,
Denise Bornhausen, Kirk & Gene Boyer, Steven Brown,
Frank Calistro, Jim Casada, Philip Dorwart, Mark Emery,
Andrew Faltynek, Ken Goff, Elliott Green, Gayle Grossman,
David Hahne, Jeff Harper, John Hunt, Jim Kyndberg,
Teresa Marrone, Kieran Moore, Matt Morgan, Betsy Nelson,
Scott Pampouch, Jessie Peine, Mike Phillips, Doris Roesch,
Michael Rostance, Cliff Santa, Steve Schenten, George Snyder,
Doug Sperry, Nathan Stausser, Keith Sutton, Kristin Tombers,
Greg Ricardo Jorge Lopes de Matos Catarrinho.

RECIPES FROM NATURE
by Kay and Bill Lindner

All photographs copyright © 2006 Bill Lindner, except
pp. 72 © Creative Publishing international

Library of Congress Cataloging-in-Publication Data

Lindner, Bill.
  Recipes from nature / Kay and Bill Lindner.
     p. cm.
  Includes index.
  ISBN 1-58923-238-0 (hard cover)
  1. Cookery (Wild foods) 2. Wild plants, Edible--North America.
3.Wildlife as food--North America. I. Lindner, Kay. II. Title.
TX751.L556 2006
641.5'63--dc22   2005023734

Recipes from Nature
CONTENTS

INTRODUCTION

Growing up in the city, my first experiences with gathering food from the outdoors was fetching cucumbers, tomatoes, and leaf lettuce for supper from my father's garden; snitching green apples from the neighbor's tree, and strawberry picking at a local farm with my mom and grandma, both award-winning canners. My grandpa was a dedicated angler and hunter, who used all of his harvest—from saving bird bones for soup, to making his own venison sausage and salami.

It was not until after college and having moved away from home that I became more interested in foods from the outdoors. I worked at a company that published cookbooks, and became exposed to common and exotic wild game and fish. I was struck by the excitement of those who hunted and fished, sharing their harvests and favorite ways to prepare them. Volunteering for taste-testing panels, hand modeling in the photos, and reading the final books—all introduced me to a level of appreciating recipes that truly were from the wild.

Bill, an outdoor and food photographer for the company, and I started working together on food/outdoor editorial pieces. We spent our free time and vacations seeking nature's edibles, people that knew a lot about them, and ideas and information for our next project. Eventually we joined our lives in matrimony and married our interests: I write, and he shoots.

Bill grew up in Chicago and moved to Brainerd, Minnesota, as a teen. His family joined the fishing industry as entrepreneurs. It wasn't until later when he discovered morel mushroom hunting that he became interested in foraging. That led to other fungi, which took him to places where he found wild leeks and fiddlehead ferns. For a while it was a frenzy every spring. Now it's a simmering passion every season.

This cookbook is the culmination of our experiences in being drawn to the outdoors, the challenge and thrill of finding food, the joy of preparation, and the gratification of having a delicious meal from nature that nourishes the body, palate, and soul.

Our general definition of recipes from nature includes foods that are seasonal, native, and locally grown. For meat, fish, and poultry, labels would include:
- "natural," raised without antibiotics, hormones, or animal proteins. Not altered with food coloring or artificial additives.
- "farm-raised" and "on-farm processing," animals are born, raised and slaughtered in the same pasture.
- "grass-fed" or "pasture-finished" animals have spent their whole lives on pasture and never fattened up with grain.
- "organic" means the animals were raised on organic feed—no antibiotics, hormones, or animal byproducts.

To our delight, we are seeing more and more connections and relationships between food producers and buyers, including co-operatives, supermarkets, farmers markets, chefs, restaurateurs, and general consumers. A wonderful trend is forming; people are responding to a higher level of expectation. They want quality ingredients; solid information on freshness and resources; and the ability to purchase local, national, and international foods. In general, the average consumer is becoming much more food savvy, not only in the arena of cooking, but also in caring about sustainable agriculture, pure food products, and the conditions and standards of our food sources.

The recipes included in this book are guidelines to savoring the finished dishes and you must feel free to respect your own taste buds. Many of the ingredients can be interchanged with other favorites. Be resourceful: the outdoors, your own garden or windowbox of herbs, farmers markets, ethnic markets, grocery stores, and co-ops all have foods you will want to try. Have fun putting together these gifts of nature; experimentation can be serendipitously successful!

Kay Lindner

Appetizers and Small Plates

For centuries, many cultures have recognized the importance of gathering before dinner to linger over small servings of various foods. To the French, *hors d'oeuvre* literally translates to "outside the main design of the meal." Starters not only serve to whet the appetite, they can serve to facilitate social interaction. The Chinese *dim sum,* means "touch the heart." And Indians refer to fried finger foods as *chat.* Conversation and companionship go hand-in-hand when it comes to nibbling.

As Spanish tapa bars and restaurants that offer sampler plates and platters pop up, the trend in sharing tastes of the season remains timeless. Yet timing is everything in taking advantage of regional treasures from the outdoors. Keeping in mind that a little goes a long way, the key is to let the fresh ingredients shine.

Pickling

A history of floods, droughts and famines taught the Chinese to stretch their food supply, as early as the third century B.C., by preserving fish, meats and vegeatables for use at another time or season. Colonial times introduced the pickle barrel. And home canning became popular in the early 1920s.

Pickling is one of the oldest preservations methods. Plain and simply, microorganisms don't like acid, which prevents or slows down food spoilage.

Depending on the vegetable, it can be fermented in brine, which takes several weeks, or quick-brined, taking only a couple of days.

Pickling fish works very well on oilier species such as herring, shad, black cod, striped bass, and chinook salmon.

Pickled Ramps
Makes 1-pint (500 ml) jar

Pickled ramps can be used for adding a piquant flavor to salads or sandwiches. Or serve them as a part of a crudités arrangement.

8 to 10 ramps (wild leeks), trimmed (green leaves intact)
¾ cup (175 ml) rice wine vinegar
¼ cup (60 ml) sugar
½ cup (125 ml) water
1 bay leaf, cracked into 2 pieces
3 juniper berries

Cut the greens off the ramp bulbs, and reserve. Put the bulbs in a 1-pint (500 ml) canning jar.

Blanch the greens in boiling water (about 30 seconds) just until limp and drain. Fold into the canning jar with the ramp bulbs.

In a small saucepan, simmer the vinegar, sugar, water, bay leaf, and juniper over low heat for 2 to 3 minutes. Pour over the ramps. Seal the jar with the lid. Store the ramps in the refrigerator for up to 3 weeks.

Hot Wild Rice and Crayfish Spread
Makes 3 cups

Serve with fresh or toasted French bread slices.

3 tablespoons (50 ml) minced garlic
¼ cup (60 ml) olive oil
1 pound (450 g) cooked crayfish tail meat
1½ cups (375 ml) cooked wild rice
2 medium red bell peppers, roasted, peeled, and diced
⅓ cup (75 ml) finely sliced scallions
⅓ cup (75 ml) chopped fresh basil
¼ cup (60 ml) sun-dried tomatoes, chopped
1½ cups (375 ml) mayonnaise
⅔ cup (150 ml) dried bread crumbs
1 tablespoon (15 ml) Tabasco sauce
1 tablespoon (15 ml) salt
1 teaspoon (5 ml) fresh lemon juice

Preheat the oven to 375°F (190°C).

Sauté the garlic in the olive oil in a small skillet over medium heat for 1 minute. Do not allow it to brown. Let the oil and garlic cool.

Combine the oil and garlic mixture with the crayfish, rice, bell peppers, scallions, basil, and sun-dried tomatoes in a large bowl. Add the mayonnaise, bread crumbs, Tabasco, salt, and lemon juice and mix together well. Transfer to a shallow baking dish.

Bake until mixture bubbles around the edges, 15 to 20 minutes. Serve hot.

Smoked Pheasant Autumn Roll

Yields 12 rolls

Smoke the pheasant or chicken legs with cherry or apple wood chips for a less intense smoke flavor. Hickory chips are too harsh for this delicate-tasting meat.

FILLING:
4 pheasant or chicken legs
Salt and pepper
4 tablespoons (60 ml) canola oil
¼ small head cabbage, julienned
½ onion, julienned
1 apple, julienned
¼ cup (60 ml) julienned celery root
1 butternut squash, peeled, seeded, and chopped
1 tablespoon (15 ml) butter
1 tablespoon (15 ml) brown sugar
⅛ teaspoon (0.5 ml) ground allspice
⅛ teaspoon (0.5 ml) ground cinnamon
2 cups (500 ml) water or chicken stock, divided

VINAIGRETTE:
1 cup (250 ml) chopped, toasted chestnuts
1 cup (250 ml) apple cider vinegar
½ onion, minced
4 leaves fresh sage, finely shredded
2 tablespoons (30 ml) sugar
1 tablespoon (15 ml) salt
2 teaspoons (10 ml) black pepper
½ cup (125 ml) olive or canola oil
12 spring roll pastry wrappers (8 inches/20.5 cm square)
Peanut oil, for deep-frying

To smoke the pheasant, season the legs with salt and pepper. Heat a large cast-iron skillet over medium-high heat with a handful of cherry or apple wood chips on one side of the pan. When the chips begin to smoke, arrange the legs on the other side of the pan. Turn off the heat and cover the pan with aluminum foil; let sit for 5 to 10 minutes. Remove meat from legs and set aside (discard skin, bones, and cartilage).

Heat 2 tablespoons (30 ml) canola oil in a large skillet over medium-high heat. Add the cabbage and onion and sauté until limp, about 5 minutes. Transfer to a large bowl and add the meat, apple, and celery root. Mix well and set aside.

To prepare the squash, heat 2 tablespoons (30 ml) canola oil in a large sauté pan over high heat. Add the squash and sauté until slightly softened. Add the butter, brown sugar, allspice, and cinnamon. Season with salt and pepper. Sauté until caramelized and soft, adding water or stock as needed (up to ½ cup/125 ml) to prevent sticking. Purée in blender, adding water or stock as needed to make a smooth purée, but not too thin. Combine squash purée with the pheasant mixture.

To make the vinaigrette to serve with the rolls, whisk together the chestnuts, vinegar, onion, sage, sugar, salt, and pepper in a small bowl. Whisk in the oil until well blended.

To assemble, take one spring roll wrap and brush with an egg wash (1 egg, 1 tablespoon water) around the borders. Evenly spread ½ cup (125 ml) of the meat and vegetable mixture in the center and roll tightly, like a cigar. Place seam-side-down to prevent the roll from opening. Repeat, using the remaining wraps and filling.

In a deep skillet, preheat peanut oil to 375°F (190°C). Add the rolls a few at a time and fry until golden brown, for 3 to 5 minutes. Drain well.

Serve the rolls hot, passing the vinaigrette on the side.

Pickled Pike

Makes 2 quarts (2 l)

Serve on crackers.

PICKLED FISH:
6 cups (1.5 l) water
1 cup (250 ml) salt
3 to 4 pounds (1.3 to 1.8 kg) boneless northern pike fillets, cut into cracker-size chunks
2 cups (500 ml) white vinegar

FLAVORINGS:
1 cup (250 ml) sugar
2 tablespoons (30 ml) pickling spice
½ clove garlic, crushed
¼ teaspoon (1 ml) white pepper
3 large onions, halved and thinly sliced
2 tablespoons (30 ml) white wine (optional)

In a plastic or ceramic bowl, combine the water and salt to make a salt brine strong enough to float an egg. Add the fish to the brine and refrigerate for 24 hours.

Drain the brine and discard. Add the vinegar. Let the fish stand in the vinegar for another 24 hours, in the refrigerator, stirring several times.

Drain the vinegar into a saucepan and return the pike chunks to the refrigerator. Add the sugar to the vinegar along with the pickling spice, garlic, and white pepper. Bring the mixture to a boil over medium heat and boil for 5 minutes, stirring occasionally.

Let stand in the refrigerator until cool.

Layer the pike chunks alternately with the onions to fill two 1-quart (1 l) canning jars, packing the jars loosely. Pour the vinegar mixture over the pike and onions to fill the jars.

Keep refrigerated and use within 60 days. Served chilled.

Pizza Cinghale

Serves 2 to 3

Cinghale means "wild boar" in Italian. This meat is often a main ingredient in specialty pasta dishes of Tuscany.

½ **pound (225 g) wild boar meat (shoulder or leg)**
1 **medium onion**
2 **ribs celery**
½ **cup (125 ml) red wine**
2 **tablespoons (30 ml) chopped fresh garlic**
1 **tablespoon (15 ml) ground ginger**
1 **tablespoon (15 ml) ground mustard**
½ **teaspoon (2.5 ml) salt**
½ **teaspoon (2.5 ml) pepper**
4 **sun-dried tomatoes**
4 **ounces (120 g) refrigerated pizza dough**
4 **ounces (120 g) goat cheese, divided**
Leaves from ½ **sprig fresh rosemary**
2 **tablespoons (30 ml) extra virgin olive oil**

Grind the wild boar, onion, and celery in meat grinder, using medium-coarse plate into a large bowl. Add the wine, garlic, ginger, mustard, salt, and pepper. Mix thoroughly. Marinate in the refrigerator for 24 hours.

Preheat the oven to 375°F (190°C).

To reconstitute the sun-dried tomatoes, cover with boiling water in a small bowl and let stand for 10 minutes. Drain well.

Roll out the pizza dough (brought to room temperature) to form a thin crust approximately 8 inches (20.5 cm) round. Place the pizza crust on a pizza stone. Crumble the boar sausage and goat cheese evenly over the crust and top with sun-dried tomatoes.

Bake for 30 to 40 minutes until crust is golden brown. Remove from oven.

To serve, cut into 6 pieces. Sprinkle with rosemary and drizzle with the olive oil.

Smoked Salmon Dip

Makes 2½ to 3 cups (600 to 720 ml)

Try serving this dip on a fish-shaped plate for a whimsical presentation. Spoon the salmon mixture on the plate and smooth to fill the shape. Use fruits and vegetables to make a fish face. Cut maraschino cherries to make lips, a sliced onion center and food coloring to make an eye, and a red or green bell pepper sliced lengthwise works for a gill. Place dill weed in a small, zippered plastic bag and cut a small hole in the bottom corner. Use like a cake decorator icing bag to draw a lateral line and parr markings.

If you are not using home-smoked salmon, look for smoked wild Alaskan, king, coho, or sockeye. These fish have a strong, wonderful smoked flavor. Grilled wild salmon can be mixed with smoked salmon to extend the recipe.

1 **pound (450 g) boneless smoked salmon**
3 **heaping tablespoons (50 ml) mayonnaise**
2 **tablespoons (30 ml) honey**
½ **teaspoon (2 ml) cayenne pepper**
1 **tablespoon (15 ml) chopped fresh dill**
1 **(10-ounce/296 g) jar sweet pickle relish**

In a medium-size bowl, mix together the smoked salmon and mayonnaise. Stir in the honey, cayenne, dill and relish. Combine the mixture with a fork until thoroughly mixed. Or process the mixture in food processor for a smoother texture.

Chill before serving.

Morel Mushrooms

Slightly nutty in taste, morels are widely considered the most prized of wild mushrooms. Warmer weather, humidity, and gentle rains serenade the awakening earth, pregnant with life. Then, this elusive queen of spring emerges in her own time, elegantly posed for only about two weeks. Those who treasure the sight of morels and the novelty of finding them will spend many an hour in search of them.

Common varieties include yellow, gray, black, and half-free morels. Because of their unusual variations in color, shape, and size, each is a challenge to identify. But each is a delight, both in the woods and on the plate.

Tempura Morels with Walleye Stuffing
Serves 4 to 6

CANDIED PECANS:
½ cup (125 ml) pure maple syrup
1 tablespoon (15 ml) butter
1 cup (250 ml) pecans
Cayenne pepper (optional)
Salt

VINAIGRETTE:
¼ cup (60 ml) balsamic vinegar
1 shallot, minced
1 tablespoon (15 ml) coarse-ground
   mustard
1 teaspoon (5 ml) sugar
¼ cup (60 ml) olive oil
Pinch of salt
Cracked pepper

FILLING:
8 ounces (225 g) cooked, flaked
   walleye
1 tablespoon (15 ml) olive oil
½ small onion, diced
1 rib celery, diced
1 clove garlic, diced
2 tablespoons (30 ml) mayonnaise

1 tablespoon (15 ml) dry mustard
2 teaspoons (10 ml) chopped fresh dill
Salt and pepper
12 to 16 fresh morel mushrooms,
   cut in halves lengthwise

TEMPURA BATTER:
3 cups (750 ml) cake flour
¾ cup (175 ml) cornstarch
2 teaspoons (10 ml) baking soda
1 teaspoon (5 ml) kosher salt
Chilled sparkling water

FINAL ASSEMBLY:
Oil, for deep-frying
Greens
Olive oil
Fresh lemon juice
Salt
Shaved Parmesan cheese

To make the candied pecans, preheat the oven to 350°F (180°C). Heat the maple syrup in an ovenproof skillet over medium-high heat until bubbly. Stir in the butter and simmer for 1 minute. Add the pecans and mix until coated. Bake for 5 to 10 minutes, until maple syrup crystallizes and loses its glossy appearance. Remove from pan. Let cool.

To make the vinaigrette, whisk together the vinegar, shallot, mustard, and sugar in a small bowl. Whisk in the olive oil in a slow, steady stream until fully blended. Season with salt and pepper to taste.

To make the filling, steam or poach the walleye fillet until the fish flakes easily, about 5 to 6 minutes. Flake into small pieces and let cool in the refrigerator.

Heat the oil in a large skillet over medium heat. Add the onion, celery, and garlic and sauté until soft. Let cool.

Combine the cooled fish and sautéed vegetables in a medium bowl. Mix in the mayonnaise, mustard, and dill. Season with salt and pepper to taste. Fill the mushroom halves with the walleye mixture.

To make the tempura batter, combine the flour, cornstarch, baking soda, and salt in a medium bowl. Add enough sparkling water to give the batter the consistency of cream.

Preheat 1½ inches (3.8 cm) of oil in a heavy-bottom skillet to 350°F (180°C). Dip each filled morel half in the tempura batter and add, a few at a time, to the hot oil. Fry until golden and crispy, 4 minutes. Drain well.

To serve, dress the greens with olive oil, lemon juice, and salt. Arrange on individual plates and top with the mushrooms. Drizzle with the vinaigrette and garnish with the candied nuts and Parmesan cheese.

Duck Chestnut Rumake

Makes 24 appetizers

MARINADE:
1 cup (250 ml) tawny port or any full-bodied red wine
¼ cup (60 ml) soy sauce
2 tablespoons (30 ml) dark sesame oil
½ cup (125 ml) fresh peeled and grated ginger
1 clove garlic, minced

DUCK:
1 pound (450 g) duck breasts
1 pound (450 g) lean and meaty sliced bacon
3 (8-ounce/225 g) cans water chestnuts (about 24 chestnuts),
   rinsed and drained

To make the marinade, whisk together the port, soy sauce, sesame oil, ginger, and garlic in a mixing bowl. Add the meat and marinate in the refrigerator for at least 2 hours, up to overnight.

Pound the meat with a meat pounder until flat. Cut the duck into 1-inch (2.5 cm) square pieces. Cut the bacon strips into halves. With your fingertips, hold together a piece of duck meat and a water chestnut. Wrap a strip of bacon around both and secure with toothpick. Repeat until all of the duck is used. Brush with the marinade.

Broil for 5 to 10 minutes until bacon is crisp.

Serve immediately.

Leek and Cheese Tiny Tarts

Makes 18 tarts

These tarts are small in size, but delightfully complex in flavor. You get the classic nutty taste from the Gruyère, a semi-hard cheese originally from Switzerland, bumped up with the tangy feta, a crumbly, milky, and piquant cheese that originated in Greece. The garlic and leek onion sauté bring the flavors together.

2 tablespoons (30 ml) unsalted butter
3 leeks (or substitute scallions or shallots), trimmed
   and minced
3 cloves garlic, minced
Salt and pepper
Frozen puff pastry sheets
3 ounces (5 tablespoons/80 g) feta (or substitute goat
   cheese), crumbled
6 ounces (10 tablespoons/170 g) cave-aged Gruyère
   (or substitute a robust Swiss or Gouda), grated
¼ cup (60 ml) chopped fresh chives
Balsamic vinegar

Melt the butter in a large skillet over medium heat. Add the leeks and garlic and sauté until translucent, about 5 minutes, blending salt and pepper to taste.

Preheat the oven to 400˚F (200˚C).

Cut out 18 round pastry pieces. Place each one over a muffin cup and, with your thumb and fingertips, gently press down into the cup to form a tart shell. In each tart shell, place about 1 teaspoon (5 ml) of feta and 1½ tablespoons (25 g) of the sautéed leek mixture. Top with the Gruyère and chives.

Bake for 12 to 14 minutes until pastry is golden brown. Cool slightly, then transfer to plates.

Drizzle the perimeter of each plate with balsamic vinegar for flavor and a finished look, and serve.

Shiitake Spring Rolls

Makes 24 rolls

These spring rolls have a distinct Japanese twist: Fresh shiitake mushrooms bring a savory and assertive flavor as a substitute for the meat or seafood usually featured.

MUSHROOMS:
1/4 cup (60 ml) water
2 tablespoons (30 ml) soy sauce
2 tablespoons (30 ml) mirin
2 tablespoons (30 ml) sugar
7 to 8 shiitake mushrooms, stems removed, caps thinly sliced

SPRING ROLLS:
6 ounces (170 g) rice vermicelli
2 cups (500 ml) shredded lettuce
1 cup (250 ml) shredded carrots
12 (9-inch/23 cm) rice spring roll wrappers
Thai basil leaves

LEMON-MISO SAUCE:
Juice of 1 lemon
2 tablespoons (30 ml) miso
2 tablespoons (30 ml) dark sesame oil
1 Thai chile, seeded and finely minced

To prepare the mushrooms, mix together the water, soy sauce, mirin, and sugar in a small saucepan. Add the mushrooms. Bring to a boil over medium-high heat and boil until most of the liquid has evaporated, about 15 minutes. Set aside.

To prepare the spring rolls, soak the rice vermicelli in hot water for 10 minutes. Drain well. Blot the surface moisture off the vermicelli and mushrooms. Mix with the lettuce and carrots in a mixing bowl.

To assemble the spring rolls, place the wrappers, one at a time, for about 3 minutes or until flexible, in a large pan filled with about 1 inch (2.5 cm) of hot water. Stack the soaked wrappers and wrap in a damp towel.

Prepare another damp towel to use as a work surface. Carefully remove a wrapper from the stack and place on the work surface. Working quickly so wrapper stays damp (but not wet), place a handful of the noodle mixture, squeezed into a log shape, at the lower third of the wrapper (as you would for a burrito). Place a few basil leaves on top. Roll the short side of the wrapper around one side of the log. Fold over the sides. Then complete by rolling up the roll with the remaining long end of the wrapper. Remove to serving plate and cover. Continue with the remaining wrappers and filling. With a wet, sharp knife, slice each roll in half with a diagonal cut.

To prepare the sauce, mix together the lemon juice, miso, sesame oil, and chile. Serve as a dipping sauce with the rolls. Serve immediately.

Smoked Fish Dip

Makes 2-1/2 to 3 cups (600 to 720 ml)

Serve with a variety of crackers.

1-1/2 cups (375 ml) crumbled smoked fish
1/2 cup (125 ml) buttermilk
8 ounces (225 g) mascarpone cheese or cream cheese
1/4 cup (60 ml) minced shallots or onions
1 stalk celery, minced
1 tablespoon (15 ml) fresh dill, finely snipped
1 teaspoon (5 ml) paprika
1 teaspoon (5 ml) dark balsamic vinegar
1/2 teaspoon (2 ml) fresh lemon juice
Sea salt and cracked black pepper

Put the smoked fish in a large nonreactive bowl and add buttermilk. Cover and chill for at least 30 minutes.

Stir in the mascarpone, shallots, celery, dill, paprika, vinegar, lemon juice, and salt and pepper to taste. Cover and chill for 2 to 3 hours, until flavors have married. Serve chilled.

Pesto Panfish Roll-Ups
Makes 12 hors d'oeuvres

PESTO:
3 tablespoons (50 ml) pine nuts or skinned, roasted chestnuts
3 medium cloves garlic, peeled
½ teaspoon (2 ml) salt
1 cup (250 ml) packed fresh basil leaves
1 cup (250 ml) packed fresh parsley leaves
½ cup (125 ml) extra virgin olive oil
Grated zest of 1 lemon

12 small fish fillets, such as perch, crappie, or bluegills
   (2 to 3 ounces/56 to 84 g each)

SAUCE:
½ cup (125 ml) unsalted butter
1 tablespoon (15 ml) crushed red pepper flakes
1 tablespoon (15 ml) brined capers
Freshly ground black pepper
Grated zest of 1 lemon

To make the pesto, pulse the pine nuts, garlic, and salt in a food processor until finely ground. Gradually add the basil, parsley, and olive oil. Stir in the zest of 1 lemon. You should have about 1 cup (250 ml).

Preheat the broiler to 350°F (180°C). Brush a baking sheet with unsalted butter.

Spread each fillet with pesto. Roll up and secure with toothpick. Arrange on the prepared baking sheet and set aside.

To make the sauce, melt the butter in a small saucepan over medium heat. Add the red pepper flakes, capers, pepper and stir for 5 minutes. Fold in the zest of the second lemon and set aside.

Broil the fish 4 to 5 inches (10 to 13 cm) away from heat element for 2 to 3 minutes. Lightly drizzle the butter sauce over fish. Serve immediately.

Buckwheat Blini with Smoked Trout

Makes 40 appetizers

Buckwheat has a long tradition as an Asian and Eastern European food staple. The plant, which is not a grasslike wheat, yields seeds that are ground into flour for making noodles, among other uses. Nutty and nutritious, buckwheat flour also makes a sturdy platform for this tasty pancakelike treat, made light in texture through the use of yeast and beaten egg whites.

BLINI:
1½ cups (375 ml) buckwheat flour
1 cup (250 ml) all-purpose flour
1 tablespoon (15 ml) sugar
1 teaspoon (5 ml) salt
1 tablespoon (15 ml) active dry yeast
1 cup (250 ml) lukewarm milk (95°F/35°C)
5 medium eggs, separated, at room temperature
½ cup (125 ml) unsalted butter, melted
¾ cup (175 ml) Pilsner beer or any light lager
¼ teaspoon (1 ml) cream of tartar
Oil

PICKLED RED ONIONS:
1 medium red onion, very thinly sliced into rings
¾ cup (175 ml) seasoned rice wine vinegar
1 tablespoon (15 ml) chopped fresh dill
½ teaspoon (2 ml) mustard seed
1 cup (250 ml) sour cream
1 pound (450 g) boneless smoked trout, cut into 1-inch (2.5 cm) cubes
Dill sprigs for garnish

To prepare the blini batter, combine the flours, sugar, and salt in a large bowl. In another bowl, sprinkle the yeast on the warm milk. Whisk together the egg yolks and melted butter, then combine with the milk mixture. Add the beer and mix again. Make a well in flour mixture and stir in the milk mixture to make a batter.

In a large mixing bowl, beat the egg whites until foamy. Add the cream of tartar and continue beating until soft peaks form. Fold into the batter.

Cover and let rise in a warm place for 1½ hours.

Meanwhile, prepare the pickled onions. In a large strainer over a sink, slowly pour 4 cups (1 l) of boiling water over the onion rings. Immediately transfer the onions to a bowl and add the vinegar, dill, and mustard seed. Cover and refrigerate for 1 hour.

To cook the blini, preheat a lightly oiled skillet until very hot (water droplets will skitter when hot enough). Using a ⅛-cup (30 ml) measure for each blini, pour the batter into the skillet to make several blini. Cook for 1 minute on each side. Set aside and keep warm. Continue until all the batter is used.

To serve, top each blini appetizer with a teaspoon or two (5 to 10 ml) of sour cream, a piece of smoked fish, a few rings of drained pickled onion, and a sprig of dill.

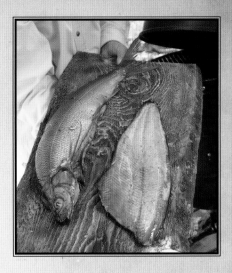

Smoking

Preparing food in a smoker comes close to the old-time barbecue taste of the South and Southwest. Sure, classic pork, beef, and chicken recipes are lip-smacking good; but smoked fish is in a category all its own. It mysteriously takes on a golden hue or mahogany color, an earthy perfume, succulent flavor and flakiness that no meat can claim. Salmon, with its higher oil content, lends itself well to absorbing the flavors of smoke cookery without drying out.

Smoke cookery is reminiscent of the slower pace of times gone by— you get to wait. Its very nature encourages you to invite friends, start in the afternoon and let the smoke unveil a leisurely dinner into the evening.

It seems there are as many ways to smoke fish as there are bodies of water to catch them. You may as well relax your state of mind, learn as you go, and take a few notes. Most important of all, pause to enjoy the quiet hissing of the wood and the unique process of smoking.

Breakfast and Brunch

One of life's small treasures is to revel in a long, luxurious breakfast feast. It is synonymous with sleeping in, inhaling the smell of brewing coffee, and squeezing sweet oranges for juice. And then come the golden waffles sprinkled with sliced strawberries, French toast laced with vanilla bean, or pancakes with whipped butter and pure maple syrup. There should, of course, be bacon bubbling in the cast-iron skillet, or some venison link sausages nestled in a pan.

Foods from nature also easily fold into a leisurely brunch. Fruit added to cereal or tossed into the blender for a drink adds a healthy component. The first chives of spring, freshly snipped, give an egg that special something. A small collection of herbs and mushrooms adds dimension to breakfast potatoes or makes an egg dish a masterpiece. Let your imagination forage through the field of possibilities.

Wild Asparagus Frittata
Serves 2 to 4

6 tablespoons (90 ml) olive oil, divided
6 shallots, thinly sliced
1 tablespoon (15 ml) balsamic vinegar
1 tablespoon (15 ml) water
½ teaspoon (2 ml) brown sugar
1 potato, very thinly sliced
2 cloves garlic, minced
2 ounces (60 g) wild asparagus, chopped (8 spears)
¼ cup (60 g) artichokes, diced
¼ cup (60 g) cherry tomatoes, cut in half

4 medium eggs, beaten
2 tablespoons (30 ml) wild parsley
¼ cup (60 ml) crumbled goat cheese
Frisée lettuce, or other wild greens
1 tablespoon (15 ml) fresh lemon juice
Salt and pepper

Heat 2 tablespoons (30 ml) of the olive oil in a large skillet over high heat. Add the shallots and sauté until seared crisp, about 5 minutes. Reduce the heat to low, add the balsamic vinegar and water and cook, stirring to deglaze the pan. Add the brown sugar. Cook gently for 20 minutes, stirring frequently to prevent the mixture from sticking or burning. Add moisture if necessary, by adding equal parts of water and balsamic vinegar in small quantities.

In another large skillet, heat 2 tablespoons (30 ml) olive oil (enough to coat the bottom of the pan) over high heat. Add the potato slices and cook until crisp on both sides, but do not burn. Remove the potatoes with a slotted spatula and set aside on paper towels. Wipe out the skillet.

Return the skillet to medium-high heat. In new oil (2 table-spoons/30 ml) or enough to coat pan bottom, sauté garlic for 2 minutes. Add asparagus, artichokes, and tomatoes, and sauté for about 5 minutes, until tender.

Preheat the oven to 375°F (190°C).

In a nonstick, 9-inch (23 cm) round pan make a layer of the potato slices and half the sautéed vegetables. Beat the eggs with the parsley and pour in. Top with the remaining sautéed ingredients and goat cheese.

Bake for 20 minutes until golden brown.

Toss the frisée with lemon juice and olive oil and season with salt and pepper.

To serve, make a nest of the dressed greens on each serving plate. Place 2 or 3 medium wedges of frittata on top of one another next to the greens.

Billy's Basted Eggs
Serves 4

Free-range chicken eggs have an intense orange-yellow yolk. They are rich and surprisingly flavorful, with a hint of chlorophyll. Busha Browne's Tomato Love Apple Sauce is made with tomato, cane sugar, peppers, vinegar, and herbs. It can be found at high-end grocery stores and specialty food stores. It gives this dish a piquant finish.

8 strips bacon
3 tablespoons (50 ml) olive oil
½ cup (125 ml) minced shallots or onions
3 to 5 cloves garlic, minced
3 tablespoons (45 ml) unsalted butter
4 large eggs
8 orange slices
Salad greens
8 slices whole wheat or rye bread, toasted
Busha Browne's Tomato Love Apple Sauce
¼ cup (60 ml) fresh chopped chives
½ cup (125 ml) finely shredded cheese, such as a sharp cheddar, a nutty Swiss, or a robust blue

Fry the bacon in a large skillet over medium-high heat until crisp, about 10 minutes. Drain on paper towels. Crumble when cool enough to handle.

In a separate pan, heat the oil over medium heat. Add the shallots and sauté for 5 minutes. Add the garlic and sauté for 5 more minutes. Remove garlic and shallot pieces from the pan and set aside.

Return the pan to medium-low heat, and melt 3 tablespoons (45 ml) butter to cover the bottom of the pan. When butter is completely melted and hot, break the eggs into the pan. Cover for 1 minute to let the whites set and the yolks start to cook. Spoon melted butter from the pan onto yolk and cover; repeat a few times until the delicate white film is formed. The eggs should be fully cooked within 6 minutes.

To serve, arrange two orange slices on beds of salad greens on four plates. Using a spatula, carefully separate the four eggs in the pan and transfer one onto each plate. Serve with toast and 2 strips of bacon. Drizzle the sides of the plate with a little Love Apple Sauce. Garnish with chives and cheese.

Red Flannel Hash with Poached Quail Eggs

Serves 6 to 8

The sound of the quail is a soothing coo and whistle. Females are speckled and grayish, like their egg shells. Their eggs have a superb tasting yolk and are adaptable to any recipe.

4 cups (1 l) peeled, diced Yukon Gold potatoes
2 cups (500 ml) medium beets, peeled and diced
7 slices smoked bacon, diced
1 onion, finely diced
5 cloves garlic, minced
Chopped fresh chives, to garnish
12 to 16 quail eggs

Boil the potatoes and beets in a large pot of heavily salted water until tender, about 20 minutes. Drain well. Set aside.

Fry the bacon in a large skillet over medium-high heat until crisp, about 5 minutes. Remove the bacon with a slotted spoon and drain on paper towels.

Return the skillet to medium-high heat, add the onion and sauté until limp, about 3 minutes. Add the garlic and sauté for 2 minutes more, until the onion has colored. Add prepared vegetables adn bacon. Warm until juices have thickened, and then garnish with chives.

Fill a saucepan with water and bring to a boil. Reduce the heat to maintain a simmer. Splash a little vinegar into the pan; this weill keep the eggwhites firm. Carefully add the eggs. Cook the eggs until the whites are set and the centers still soft, 2 minutes. Remove with a slotted spoon and drain.

To serve, place a small ring mold (a napkin holder can work as a substitute) in the center of the each plate and spoon the hash into the mold, pushing down with the back of your spoon. Top each serving with two eggs and serve immediately.

Eggs

There is much folklore and tradition surrounding eggs. For example, the number of pleats in a tall, white chef's hat traditionally represented the number of egg preparation methods he or she had mastered.

Whether you purchase them or are lucky enough to harvest them in the wild, the egg is a miraculous, self-contained package from nature. It's become a true symbol of harvest and fertility.

The egg provides endless cuisine possibilities, from simple to sophisticated. And what better reason to celebrate spring than the fact that more eggs are laid during this season than any other?

Shiitake Mushrooms

The right combination of heat, humidity, and rain can result in a wondrous, early-fall harvest of these hearty, tasty mushrooms.

Originally from Japan, Shiitake are the second most cultivated mushroom in the world. They grow naturally up and down a tree's trunk, attached to the bark. In the wild, this fungus propagates and spreads from its spores.

For home cultivation, logs are inoculated by drilling holes along the wood and "planting" them with spawn. The spawn colonizes—after about 6 to 18 months—and is ready for harvesting. A typical log produces fruit for 2 to 5 years.

Creamy Artichoke-Blossom Eggs
Serves 4

Artichokes are flower buds. To take advantage of their form, a blossom presentation is a natural. This makes one big plateful of brunch, albeit mostly artichoke. The tasty cheese sauce complements both the eggs and artichoke and makes for a hearty meal. Let this dish take center stage and serve with fresh fruit and field greens.

4 medium artichokes
Juice of 1 lemon
Water
4 slices Canadian bacon
2 teaspoons (10 ml) olive, divided
8 medium eggs
½ cup (125 ml) whole milk
Salt and pepper

CHEESE SAUCE:
3 tablespoons (45 ml) butter
3 tablespoons (50 ml) all-purpose flour
1½ cups (375 ml) whole milk
¾ cup (175 ml) grated Parrano or other sharp, flavorful cheese
Salt and pepper

Wash and trim the artichokes. Place the artichokes in a deep kettle filled with 3 inches (7.5 cm) of water. Add the lemon juice and cover. Bring to a boil over medium-high heat, then reduce the heat to a simmer, and cook for 45 minutes, until the artichokes are fork-tender at the base. Turn the artichokes upside down to drain and cool.

When the artichokes are cool enough to handle, remove the stems and reserve for another use. Remove the small outer leaves at the base and discard. Gently pry open the loose outer leaves around the inner bud. Grasping firmly, twist the bud loose and discard. Scrape out the fuzzy choke with a spoon. (Preparing the artichokes up to this point can be done the night before.)

To make the sauce, melt the butter in a small saucepan over medium-high heat. Stir in the flour to form a roux. Cook for several minutes until honeycombed. Reduce the heat to medium, add the milk, and whisk until thickened. Add the cheese and continue whisking until the cheese is melted. Season to taste with salt and pepper. Set aside and keep warm.

Reheat the artichokes in a saucepan with 1 inch (2.5 cm) of water over medium heat and keep warm.

Fry the Canadian bacon in 1 teaspoon (5 ml) oil in a large sauté pan over medium-high heat for about 1 minute on each side until warmed through. Set aside and keep warm.

Beat the eggs with the milk. Add salt and pepper. Pour the remaining 1 teaspoon (5 ml) oil into a large sauté pan set over low heat. Pour in the eggs and cook, stirring occasionally with a spatula. To avoid dry eggs, remove from the heat when the eggs are set but still shiny-moist. Eggs will continue to cook off of the heat.

To assemble, place one artichoke on a large dinner plate. Press gently open until the leaves lie flat and the artichoke resembles a green sunflower. Leaves that accidentally break off can be set in place and patched with filling. Ladle 1 tablespoon (15 ml) cheese sauce on the artichoke heart, then layer a piece of Canadian bacon, followed by a mound of scrambled eggs, topped with another tablespoon of cheese sauce. Repeat to assemble the remaining artichokes.

Serve immediately.

Shiitake Mushroom Strudel
Serves 10

6 tablespoons (85 ml) butter
6 cups (1.5 l) chopped shiitake mushrooms
½ cup (125 ml) marsala or dry sherry
¼ cup (60 ml) chopped shallots
1 teaspoon (5 ml) salt
¼ teaspoon (1 ml) curry powder
1½ cups (375 ml) fresh bread crumbs
1 cup (250 ml) sour cream
1 sheet (8-ounce/225 g) puff pastry
1 medium egg
2 tablespoons (30 ml) milk

Melt the butter in a large skillet over medium heat. Add the mushrooms, marsala, shallots, salt, and curry, and cook, stirring, until the liquid is mostly gone, 10 to 15 minutes. Let cool.

Stir in the the bread crumbs and sour cream.

Preheat the oven to 350º F (180˚C).

Roll out the puff pastry to form a 16x22-inch (40.5x56 cm) rectangle. Spread the filling on the pastry, leaving a 1-inch (2.5 cm) border around the edges. Beat the egg with the milk in a small bowl and brush around the edges of the pastry. Roll up jelly-roll style, from the long side. Brush the top with the remaining egg wash.

Bake for 20 minutes, until golden. Cool slightly before slicing. Can be served warm or cold.

Wild Rice Pancakes with Apples

Serves 6

*To make this recipe you will need to make wild rice flour. Simply process
1/2 cup (125 ml) uncooked wild rice at high speed in a blender until ground
to a fine powder. Do not use a food processor.*

1¼ cups (300 ml) all-purpose flour
1 cup (250 ml) wild-rice flour
¾ cup (175 ml) sugar
2 teaspoons (10 ml) baking powder
½ teaspoon (2 ml) baking soda
½ teaspoon (2 ml) ground nutmeg
¼ teaspoon (1 ml) salt
2¾ cups (675 ml) sour cream, divided
1¼ cups (300 ml) cold water
2 medium eggs
1½ cups (375 ml) cooked wild rice
5 tablespoons (75 ml) butter, melted, divided
2 medium apples, peeled, cored, sliced ¼ inch (5 mm) thick
Maple syrup, warmed

In a large bowl, combine the all-purpose and wild-rice flours, sugar, baking
powder, baking soda, nutmeg, and salt. Sift together twice.

In another large bowl, whisk 2 cups (500 ml) of the sour cream, water, and eggs
until smooth. Whisk in the dry ingredients, mixing just until blended. Fold in the
cooked wild rice and 4 tablespoons (60 ml) of the butter. Let the batter stand for
20 minutes.

In a large skillet, heat the remaining 1 tablespoon (15 ml) butter until foamy.
Arrange the apples in a single layer in the skillet. Cook over medium heat for
1 to 2 minutes; turn the apple slices and cook just until tender, 1 to 2 minutes
longer. Keep warm.

In a large, greased skillet, cook the pancakes using ¼ cup (60 ml) batter for each
and cooking over medium heat until browned, 3 to 4 minutes on each side.

To serve, arrange the pancakes on serving plates; top with the sautéed apples
and remaining sour cream. Serve with maple syrup.

Maple Syrup

At a certain time of year, sugar
maples seem to rest within a bed-
spread of snow. With a bite still in
the air, the longer days begin to blow
a breath of vitality into the lifeblood
of these trees. Deep inside their
complex root and trunk system rests
the maple sap. Then, it quietly stirs,
with the warmth of spring to awaken
it, and "runs."

Long ago, the survival of the
Anishinabe people was contingent
upon their ability to live by the
seasons, utilizing the bounty
from woodland and water. Their
migration travels were a natural
transition between seasons and,
through necessity, maple syrup
became a food staple. This delicate,
sweet treat is still harvested and
enjoyed today.

Double Buttermilk Pancakes with Blueberry Sauce

Serves 4 to 6

3 cups (750 ml) buttermilk pancake and waffle mix
2½ cups (625 ml) buttermilk
¼ cup (60 ml) corn oil
2 medium eggs
2 percent low-fat milk (optional)

SAUCE:
¼ cup (60 ml) maple syrup
½ cup (125 ml) blueberries

To make the pancake batter, mix together the pancake mix, buttermilk, oil, and eggs until smooth with no lumps. If you like thinner pancakes, add a bit of milk to the batter.

To make the blueberry sauce, combine the maple syrup and blueberries in a glass measuring cup. Do not mix or stir. Microwave on high for 1 to 2 minutes. Do not allow the mixture to boil. Gently mix with a fork and keep warm.

To cook the pancakes, lightly butter or oil a griddle and preheat. Spoon about ⅓ cup (80 ml) batter onto the griddle for each pancake. Cook until the top of each pancake is dotted with bubbles and some of the bubbles have popped open. Turn and cook until the underside is lightly browned. Serve immediately with the blueberry sauce poured or spooned over each pancake.

Cranberry-Orange Bread

Makes 1 loaf

1 cup (250 ml) fresh or frozen cranberries
1 cup (250 ml) sugar
2 cups (500 ml) all-purpose flour
1½ teaspoons (7 ml) baking powder
½ teaspoon (2 ml) baking soda
½ teaspoon (2 ml) salt
8 to 12 fresh oranges
1 medium egg
2 tablespoons (30 ml) butter, melted

Cut each cranberry in half crosswise, not lengthwise. Sprinkle with the sugar to coat the surfaces. Let stand in a bowl overnight at room temperature.

Preheat the oven to 350°F (180°C). Grease a 9x5x3-inch (23x13x8 cm) loaf pan with solid vegetable shortening. (Do not use butter, which will prematurely brown the bottom of the loaf and make it difficult to remove from the pan.)

Sift or mix together the flour, baking powder, baking soda, and salt.

Grate the zest of 1 orange into a bowl and then squeeze fresh oranges until you have ¾ cup (175 ml) juice. (Do not use frozen concentrate.) Beat the egg and mix with orange juice and orange zest. Mix in the butter.

Pour the orange juice mixture into the dry ingredients and mix thoroughly. Fold in the cranberries and all the juices. Spoon the batter into the prepared pan.

Bake for 1 hour, or until a toothpick inserted into the center comes out clean.

Remove the pan from the oven and cool the bread in the pan on a wire rack. Use a thin knife around the sides of the pan to loosen the loaf. Let stand in the pan until warm to the touch, but not hot, and use a spatula to gently lift the loaf from one end of the pan. The bread will stick and have a tendency to break apart if it is removed when it is still hot. Fresh bread can be wrapped when cool and frozen. It keeps well for several weeks.

Artisan Cheese Plate

Serves 6

Serve the cheeses at room temperature with a nice piece of crusty bread and summer fruit. The Point Reyes blue cheese is an amazing match with a spicy, juicy tangerine. In the cool weather months, serve with Forelle or Comice pears instead of the tangerine. Bing cherries in season are a sweet complement especially to the camembert.

8 ounces (225 g) Point Reyes Original Blue Cheese, a California raw cow's milk blue cheese or similar blue cheese
8 ounces (225 g) Widmer cheddar cheese, an aged (6 years) cheddar made in Wisconsin from cow's milk, or similar aged cheddar
8 ounces (225 g) Nancy's Hudson Valley Camembert, a sheep's milk camembert made in New York, or similar sheep's milk camembert
Crackers
Crusty bread
½ cup (250 ml) toasted walnuts
3 tangerines, cut into slices
1 cup (250 ml) fresh pitted Bing cherries
2 pears, cut into slices

Serve the cheeses unwrapped, whole, and at room temperature, each with its own knife for guests to cut as they please. Accompany with your favorite crackers and a crusty French baguette, sliced and served in a basket. Serve with fruits and nuts in small bowls near the cheese board.

Morels on Crostini

Serves 6

MORELS:
8 ounces (225 g) morels
4 tablespoons (60 ml) butter
1 tablespoon (15 ml) olive oil
1 shallot, minced
2 cloves garlic, minced
¼ cup (60 ml) white wine
⅓ cup (75 ml) chicken stock or broth
¼ cup (60 ml) crème fraîche
¼ cup (60 ml) heavy cream
Finely snipped fresh herbs

CROSTINI
1 baguette, 4 to 6 hard rolls, or 8 ounces (225 g) Italian or French bread
½ cup (1 stick) (125 ml) butter, softened
1 tablespoon (15 ml) garlic powder
1 tablespoon (15 ml) onion powder
1 teaspoon (5 ml) finely cracked black pepper

Place the morels in a colander and run water over them for few minutes to rinse away surface particles and dirt. Pour 6 to 8 cups (1.5 to 2 l) of water into a large bowl and add 2 to 3 tablespoons (30 to 50 ml) of salt. Add the morels and let stand for 10 minutes, occasionally stirring. Rinse through a colander, running water over the mushrooms. Repeat until the water runs clear. Slice medium and large morels in half lengthwise; keep small ones whole. Set aside on paper towels to drain. To reconstitute the sun-dried tomatoes, cover with boiling water in a small bowl and let stand for 10 minutes. Drain well.

In a large sauté pan, melt the butter with the olive oil over medium heat. Add the shallot and sauté for 3 minutes. Add the garlic and sauté for 3 minutes. Add the morels, and sauté for 3 minutes. Add the white wine and chicken stock and simmer over low heat for 10 to 15 minutes to reduce a little. Add the crème fraîche, heavy cream, and herbs to taste. Simmer, stirring, for 3 to 5 minutes.

Preheat the broiler. Line a baking sheet with aluminum foil.

Slice the bread into appetizer-size pieces (about one-quarter the size of bread sliced for sandwiches).

Combine the butter, garlic powder, onion powder, and pepper in a small bowl. Spread on bread. Arrange butter-side-up on the prepared baking sheet. Broil for about 5 minutes, or (as ovens vary) until golden brown.

Spoon the morels over the toasted bread and serve immediately.

Side Dishes

Nature offers countless ingredients for
salad, vegetable, and starch dishes.
The tapestry of greens available from around
the country provide so many ways to make
beautiful salads or to simply garnish a plate
for color or add a fresh element.
Once you have foraged for wild vegetables,
you will always want to include them on
your table. Pasta, potato, and rice dishes
also benefit from the myriad distinct
and concentrated flavors given to us by
the natural world.

Vegetables, Salads, and Fungi

The popular fifties' "salad plate" of iceberg lettuce leaves, a scoop of cottage cheese and some pale tomato wedges has surely evolved over the years. Greens alone bring us a vast array to choose from, including micro greens, field greens, and hearty leaves.

With an increase in demand for good-quality produce, there are more and more resources available: the wild, your own garden, farmers' markets, and many supermarkets, which carry heirloom, organic, and local options.

Year-round, many of these lovely vegetables just beg to be picked and used creatively.

Chicken with Wild Rice Salad

Serves 4

1 pound (450 g) boneless, skinless chicken breast, cooked and sliced
1 cup (250 ml) cooked wild rice
¼ cup (60 ml) chopped celery
¼ cup (60 ml) thinly sliced scallions
2 to 4 tablespoons (25 to 60 ml) chopped toasted walnuts
1 tablespoon (15 ml) dried cranberries
⅔ cup (150 ml) mayonnaise
1½ teaspoons (7 ml) curry powder
1 teaspoon (5 ml) fresh lemon juice
Kosher salt and pepper
Salad greens

In a large bowl, mix together the wild rice, celery, scallions, walnuts, and cranberries. In a small bowl, stir together the mayonnaise, curry powder, and lemon juice. Add to the rice mixture and mix well. Season to taste with salt and pepper. Refrigerate at least 1 hour to blend the flavors.

To serve, arrange the salad greens on individual serving plates. Spoon the rice mixture on greens and top with a sliced chicken breast. Garnish with fresh chives. Serve immediately.

Fiddleheads with Asian Dressing

Serves 2

2 tablespoons (30 ml) soy sauce
2 teaspoons (10 ml) dark sesame oil
2 teaspoons (10 ml) rice vinegar (optional)
1 teaspoon (5 ml) sugar
1 teaspoon (5 ml) sesame seeds
A good pinch of cayenne pepper
1 cup (250 ml) fiddleheads (Ostrich Fern coils)

Combine the soy sauce, sesame oil, vinegar, if using, sugar, sesame seeds, and cayenne in a bowl or small container; mix well. (This can be done earlier in the day; store the mixture at room temperature. If you want to prepare the dressing even more in advance, omit the sesame seeds until you're ready to serve.)

Bring a large pot of salted water to a boil. Add the fiddleheads. Return to a gentle boil, and cook for 10 minutes. Drain and refresh immediately with lots of cold water. Drain a second time and refresh immediately with lots of cold water.

In a mixing bowl, combine the fiddleheads and dressing, stirring to coat. Let stand for at least 10 minutes, or as long as an hour, before serving. Serve at room temperature.

Braised Spinach

Serves 2

¼ cup (60 ml) unsalted butter
2 tablespoons (30 ml) dry white wine
1 pound (450 g) fresh spinach, tough stems discarded

In large skillet, melt butter over medium heat. Stir in wine. Add the spinach and stir frequently until spinach is wilted. Remove from the heat and serve immediately.

Fiddlehead Ferns

Nearly all ferns have a stage of growth when they are a tightly coiled young shoot, resembling their namesake head of a violin. There are many look-alikes but only one species is edible: fiddleheads from the Ostrich Fern. At this early stage, they have a strong chlorophyll flavor. Some say they taste like asparagus; some say a hint of green beans.

These young shoots appear in late June or July, often on moist, wooded slopes. They are best when harvested as they first appear, just a few inches (centimeters) above the ground. Fiddleheads are in their coiled form for only about two weeks before they unfurl into graceful greenery.

Tip: Be sure to cook fiddleheads thoroughly to avoid any food-borne illness.

Watercress

If ever a food deserved a celebration, it's watercress! In June, many people observe National Watercress Week by visiting areas where this lush green is abundant, ready to eat fresh, or for trying a new recipe.

Watercress is a dark green, delicate, leafy plant with fine white roots. Eaten raw, it has a peppery or tangy taste. It can really enhance an old, stand-by salad, appetizer, or sandwich. Native to Europe and the Mediterranean region, this perennial herb can be found year-round along streams and in shallow springs throughout North America.

Watercress Salad
Serves 6

3 cups (750 ml) tender greens (baby romaine or field greens)
1½ cups (375 ml) watercress, tough stems removed
2 tablespoons (30 ml) extra virgin olive oil
2½ teaspoons (12 ml) white wine vinegar or light balsamic vinegar
½ teaspoon (2 ml) onion powder
¼ teaspoon (1 ml) garlic powder

Toss the greens in a large salad bowl.

Combine the olive oil, vinegar, onion powder, and garlic powder in a jar or small bowl. Shake or stir to emulsify. Pour the mixture over greens and toss well. Serve immediately.

Chard Sauté with Blue Cheese
Serves 4 to 6

¼ cup (60 ml) butter, softened
1 cup (250 ml) diced white onion
2 tablespoons (30 ml) minced fresh garlic
1 tablespoon (15 ml) kosher salt
Pinch of ground nutmeg
2 pounds (900 g) fresh ruby or red Swiss chard, julienned
2 cups (500 ml) julienned red bell pepper
Blue cheese, crumbled

In a large pot, melt the butter over medium heat. Add the onion and sauté until translucent, about 5 minutes. Add the garlic, salt, and nutmeg. Stir lightly, then add the chard and peppers and cook until just hot and wilted, about 2 minutes.

Serve hot, with the crumbled blue cheese as a garnish.

Pecorino Packets
Serves 6

1 medium bunch ruby or red Swiss chard
12 ounces (330 g) Italian pecorino cheese with truffles, cut into 2-ounce (60 g) pieces (or substitute boschetto al tartufo, a cow's milk cheese)
¼ cup (60 ml) butter
2 ounces (30 ml) grated Parmesan cheese

Bring a large pot of salted water to a boil. Add the chard and blanch until wilted, about 1 minute. Remove the chard from the water and lay flat on dry towels to cool.

Separate the leaves into two large pieces along the center rib, removing the rib and discarding. Cut the halved leaves into two more pieces. Fold each quarter piece of chard around a piece of pecorino, forming a packet. Press the weight of your hand on the packet to close tightly.

Melt the butter in a large sauté pan over medium heat. Add pecorino packets and cook about 5 minutes. Turn and cook on other side about 2 minutes or until packets are soft and butter has turned a nutty brown.

To serve, arrange the packets on a plate. Pour the browned butter over the top and garnish with the Parmesan cheese.

Cêpes in Cream on Polenta with Wilted Greens
Serves 8

The king bolete, also known as cêpes to the French, is one of the meatiest, most coveted of fall mushrooms.

POLENTA:
4 cups (1 l) chicken broth or stock, divided
1 teaspoon (5 ml) sea salt
1½ cups (375 ml) coarsely ground cornmeal
½ cup (125 ml) grated Parmesan cheese

MUSHROOM MIXTURE:
¼ cup (60 ml) unsalted butter
1 pound (450 g) fresh king bolete (or other fresh mushroom), cleaned and diced
2 shallots, minced
½ cup (125 ml) dry white wine
1 cup (250 ml) half-and-half
Sea salt

GREENS:
1 tablespoon (15 ml) olive oil
1 teaspoon (5 ml) sugar
½ teaspoon (2 ml) sea salt
¼ teaspoon (1 ml) nutmeg
12 cups (3 l) assorted winter greens (kale, collards, or Swiss chard), tough stems removed, chopped

Preheat the oven to 350°F (180°C). Butter a 9x5x3-inch (23x13x8 cm) loaf pan.

To make the polenta, in a medium saucepan, bring 2 cups (500 ml) stock to a boil with the salt. In a large glass measuring cup, combine the remaining 2 cups (500 ml) stock with the cornmeal. Pour the cornmeal mixture into the boiling stock; return to a boil. Reduce the heat, cover, and simmer for 15 minutes. Stir in the cheese. Pour into the prepared loaf pan. Reserve any extra polenta for another use.

Bake for 30 minutes.

Meanwhile, prepare the mushrooms. In a large pan, melt the butter over medium-high heat until hot but not smoking. Add the mushrooms and shallots and sauté until the mushrooms have browned, about 5 minutes. Add the wine and cook until the wine is almost evaporated. Add the cream and heat until slightly thickened. Salt to taste. Set aside and keep warm.

To prepare the greens, heat the oil in 5-quart (5 l) saucepan over medium-high heat. Add the sugar, salt, and nutmeg and sauté for 1 minute. Stir in the greens, cover, and cook until softened, about 7 minutes.

When the polenta is baked, invert entire loaf and remove from pan. Cool slightly before slicing into eight ¾-inch (2 cm) pieces.

To serve, spoon some greens over each slice of polenta. Spoon the mushroom mixture over the greens. Serve warm.

Eggplant Misoyaki
Serves 8

Eggplants come in many shapes, sizes, and colors. This more or less traditional Japanese recipe features one of the smaller, longer Asian eggplants, but you may substitute the large European variety by slicing it into rounds instead.

¾ cup (175 ml) miso
3 tablespoons (50 ml) mirin (sweet cooking rice wine)
2 tablespoons (30 ml) sugar
2 tablespoons (30 ml) sake
2 tablespoons (30 ml) fresh lemon juice
1 teaspoon (5 ml) grated fresh peeled ginger
1 teaspoon (5 ml) dark sesame oil
8 medium Asian eggplants, sliced in half lengthwise and scored diagonally, or Italian eggplants, sliced into rounds and scored
¼ cup (60 ml) water, or more as needed

Mix together the miso, mirin, sugar, sake, lemon juice, ginger, and sesame oil in a small bowl. Spread thinly with a knife onto the scored face of each eggplant. Cover and marinate overnight in refrigerator. Bring to room temperature before grilling.

Prepare a hot fire in a charcoal grill or preheat a gas grill to approximately 400°F (200°C).

Scrape the miso mixture from the eggplants with a knife, reserving the miso in a bowl. Add enough water to thin the miso mixture to a basting consistency, and brush a thin coating onto each scored face.

Place the eggplants on the grill, scored side up. Cover and grill on one side only for 10 minutes, until flesh is softened and eggplant no longer retains its original shape.

To serve, transfer the eggplants to a serving platter. Serve at room temperature.

Spring Refresher

Serves 4

1 pound (450 g) asparagus, cut into 2-inch (5 cm) pieces
4 ounces (120 g) fiddlehead ferns (ostrich fern coils)
1 tablespoon (15 ml) olive oil
12 ramps (wild leeks), bulb and greens
3 ounces (90 g) shiitake mushrooms, stems discarded and caps sliced
3 cloves garlic, thinly sliced
Salt and pepper
4 ounces (120 g) goat cheese, crumbled

Bring a large pot of salted water to a boil. Add the asparagus and blanch for 2 to 4 minutes, until the spears are just barely tender. Remove the asparagus from the water with a slotted spoon and plunge into a bowl of ice water to cool. Drain well.

Return the water to a boil. Add the fiddleheads and blanch for 10 minutes. Before rinsing, use your thumb and forefinger to rub the coiled parts back and forth to loosen the brown papery leaves (a well-fitted rubber glove is helpful). Drain well.

Heat the oil in a large skillet over medium heat. Add the ramps and cook for 2 to 4 minutes, until tender. Add the mushrooms and cook for another 2 to 4 minutes, until tender. Add the garlic and cook for 2 minutes. Add the asparagus and fiddlehead ferns and cook for another 2 minutes, or until heated through. Season with salt and pepper.

Top with crumbled goat cheese and serve.

Rosemary Garlic Squash

Serves 4

2 medium squashes (acorn, carnival, or delicata)
1 head garlic, roasted
1 tablespoon (15 ml) fresh rosemary, snipped finely
1/3 cup (75 ml) chicken stock or broth

Preheat the oven to 350°F (180°C),

Cut the squash in half lengthwise. Scoop out seeds and membranes and discard. Wrap individual halves in aluminum foil.

Cut the top third off the garlic to expose the cloves. Wrap in aluminum foil.

Roast the squash and garlic for about 1 hour, until they are are soft and tender.

Carefully unwrap the squash and spoon the contents of the shells into a large bowl. Discard the shells. Put half of the squash in a mini food processor and add 6 roasted garlic cloves (reserve the remainder for another use), the rosemary, and chicken stock. Purée and return the remaining squash to the bowl. Using a fork, mash together the purée and return to the bowl.

Serve hot.

Wild Leeks

The leek is an ancient vegetable that is found wild and cultivated in North America from north to south and coast-to-coast.

In spring, colonies of wild leeks often form large areas of ground cover, sometimes just a small, random patch.

Leeks resemble scallions and have a strong garlicky onion flavor. Raw or cooked, the bulbs are the most commonly eaten part, but the leaves are edible too. Leeks are quite popular in French cooking as a flavoring in soups.

Tip: Rinse well and keep the bulb pointed downward to draw out any mud or sand still present from harvesting.

Mâche Salad

Serves 4

Mâche, also known as lamb's lettuce, is a wonderful salad green that has a mild nuttiness and a gentle sweetness. A bright green and sturdy leaf, it has a higher nutritional value than most other salad greens. It's easy to grow in the home garden, but isn't grown commercially because the low-growing green must be hand-harvested.

Manchego is a hard, dry sheep's milk cheese from Spain that is available at specialty cheese counters. Substitute Parmesan if manchego is unavailable.

ROASTED VEGETABLES:
6 baby beets, red and yellow, well scrubbed and cut
  into quarters
12 baby carrots, peeled, greens removed to within ¼ inch
  (6 mm) of top
1 red jalapeño, roasted, peeled, and finely chopped
1 clove garlic, minced
1 teaspoon (5 ml) sea salt
2 tablespoons (30 ml) olive oil

VINAIGRETTE:
Juice of 2 limes
1 tablespoon (15 ml) chopped fresh cilantro
1 teaspoon (5 ml) honey
Pinch of salt
½ cup (125 ml) olive oil

SALAD:
3 cups (750 ml) mâche
4 ounces (120 g) manchego cheese, shaved

Preheat the oven to 450° F (230°C).

To roast the vegetables and jalapeño, combine the beets, carrots, garlic, and salt in a large roasting pan. Add the oil and toss to coat. Arrange in a single layer and roast for 15 minutes. Let cool.

Once Jalapeño has cooled, peel, remove membrane and seeds and chop finely to use in vinaigrette.

To make the vinaigrette, whisk together the lime juice, jalapeño, cilantro, honey, and salt. Whisk in the oil until well blended.

To assemble the salad, arrange the mâche on salad plates and top with the roasted vegetables and cheese shavings. Dress with the vinaigrette immediately before serving.

Frisée Fennel Salad

Serves

Frisée is a member of the chicory family. Its delicate but very defined leaves are slightly bitter, a refreshing foil to the sesame oil and melon.

SALAD:
1 head frisée lettuce
½ fennel bulb, trimmed and sliced crosswise into ¼-inch
  (6 mm) slices
24 slim crescents of cantaloupe, rind and seeds removed
  (less than 1 cantaloupe)
24 medium shrimp, cooked, shelled, and chilled

VINAIGRETTE:
Juice of 1 lemon
2 tablespoons (30 ml) Pernod
½ cup (125 ml) olive oil
½ teaspoon (2 ml) dark sesame oil
1 teaspoon (5 ml) roasted sesame seeds
Salt
Pinch of sugar
Edible flowers such as nasturtiums for garnish

In a small bowl whisk together the lemon juice, Pernod, olive oil, sesame oil, sesame seeds. Whisk in salt and sugar to taste. Set aside.

On individual serving plates arrange 4 slices of cantaloupe, top with the frisée or greens and four shrimp. Drizzle with the vinaigrette and garnish with edible flowers.

Pasta, Potatoes, and Rice

The precious, concentrated flavors of wild edibles almost beckon to be spread throughout the meal. And that is certainly true of grains, rice, and root vegetables.

Each has a unique yet neutral taste; and each is adaptable to combine with a variety of foods from the wild.

Starches, an ancient staple throughout the world and often taken for granted as everyday food, act as an artist's canvas, providing a medium to blend flavors and colors of nature to create a culinary work of art.

Farro Risotto, Pesto and Poached Eggs
Serves 6

PESTO:
5 ramps (wild leeks), trimmed
⅓ cup (75 ml) salted, roasted cashews
½ cup (125 ml) olive oil
¼ teaspoon (1 ml) sugar
Salt and pepper

RISOTTO:
1 cup (250 ml) farro
½ cup (125 ml) plus 1 tablespoon (15 ml) olive oil, divided
2 tablespoons (30 ml) butter, divided
¼ cup (60 ml) chopped shallots
⅔ cup (150 ml) dry red wine
2 cups (500 ml) chicken stock or broth
2 tablespoons (30 ml) freshly grated Parmesan cheese
Salt and pepper

EGGS:
1 bunch asparagus
1 tablespoon (15 ml) vinegar
6 medium eggs

To make the pesto, combine the ramps, cashews, oil, and sugar in a food processor and blend until smooth. Season with salt and pepper to taste. Pesto keeps in the refrigerator, surface covered with plastic wrap, for 1 week.

To make the risotto, soak the farro in cold water to cover for 20 minutes. Drain, rinse.

Bring 8 cups (2 l) water to a boil in medium saucepan. Add ½ cup (125 ml) oil and the farro. Simmer for 20 minutes. Drain in strainer and rinse.

Melt 1 tablespoon (15 ml) butter with the remaining 1 tablespoon (15 ml) oil in medium saucepan over medium heat. Add the shallots and sauté for 1 minute. Add farro and wine. Simmer until almost all liquid evaporates, stirring frequently, about 5 minutes. Add chicken stock, 1 cup (250 ml) at a time and simmer until the liquid is absorbed and the farro is just tender, stirring frequently, about 14 minutes total. Stir in the cheese and the remaining 1 tablespoon (15 ml) butter. Season with salt and pepper. Keep warm.

Steam the asparagus over boiling water until tender-crisp, about 4 to 5 minutes. Season with salt and pepper to taste. Set aside and keep warm.

To poach the eggs, fill a saucepan with water and bring to a boil. Add the vinegar to keep the whites firm and reduce the heat to maintain a simmer. Carefully add the eggs. Cook the eggs until the whites are set and the centers still soft, about 3 minutes. Remove with a slotted spoon and drain.

To serve, put a mound of risotto on a plate or in a shallow bowl, make a small well on top of the risotto and carefully place a poached egg on top. Drizzle pesto around edges of the risotto and garnish with the asparagus spears. Serve immediately.

Dandelion Greens

The name dandelion comes from the French *dent de lion*, meaning "lion's tooth," a reference to the jagged-edged leaves of this noteworthy weed that grows both wild and cultivated.

The bright-green leaves have a slightly bitter, tangy flavor that adds interest to salads. They can be wilted for a warm salad or added to pasta dishes.

If you're not used to the slight bitterness, cook them with sweet vegetables, especially sliced carrots and parsnips. Boiling dandelions in one or more changes of water also makes them milder.

Though they're available until winter in some regions, the best, most tender dandelion greens are found in early spring, before the plant begins to flower.

Early spring is also the time to harvest the crown—just above the root, where the leaves are attached. It can be sautéed, pickled, or added to cooked vegetable dishes. The roots can be eaten as vegetables or roasted and ground to make root "coffee."

Spaghetti with Ramps
Serves 2

6 ounces (170 g) spaghetti
Kosher salt and freshly ground pepper
10 tablespoons (150 ml) extra virgin olive oil, plus more to serve
¾ teaspoon (4 ml) finely chopped peeled fresh ginger
½ teaspoon (2 ml) finely chopped jalapeño
2 cups (500 ml) sliced ramps (wild leeks), trimmed into ¼-inch (6 mm) pieces
1 clove garlic, finely chopped
1 teaspoon (5 ml) butter
½ teaspoon (2 ml) finely chopped lemon zest
1 tablespoon (15 ml) grated Parmesan cheese, plus more to serve

Bring a large pot of salted water to a boil. Add the spaghetti and cook until *al dente,* according to the package directions. Drain well. Season with salt and pepper.

Meanwhile, heat the oil in a 10-inch (25 cm) sauté pan over medium heat. Add the ginger and jalapeño and sauté for 10 seconds, or until tender. Do not brown. Add the ramps and sauté for 10 seconds, or until just wilted. Add the garlic and sauté for 5 seconds. Be careful not to brown or burn.

Remove from the heat. Stir in the butter, lemon zest, and Parmesan. Add the pasta and toss. Drizzle with a little more oil and add more Parmesan, if desired. Serve immediately.

Chanterelles with Mashed New Potatoes
Serves 6

This heavenly side dish is prepared with dried chanterelles, the faintly apricot-scented yellow-orange trumpet mushroom that graces woodlands in late summer to early fall. They are becoming easier to find commercially in their dried form, so snap them up the next time you see them. They have a subtle wild flavor that is superior.

3 pounds (1⅓ kg) new potatoes (Yukon Gold, Russian Fingerlings, or other creaming variety), well scrubbed
1 tablespoon (15 ml) coarse sea salt
½ cup (125 ml) unsalted butter, at room temperature, divided
2 tablespoons (30 ml) minced shallot
2 cups (500 ml) fresh chanterelle mushrooms, cleaned and chopped or 1 cup (250 ml) dried chanterelles, soaked in hot water for 10 minutes and drained
Salt and white pepper
½ cup (125 ml) half-and-half

Put the potatoes in a large pot and add enough cold water to cover them. Bring to a boil over medium-high heat. Turn down the heat to simmer, add sea salt, and cook for 25 to 30 minutes, until fork tender. Drain well.

Meanwhile, melt ¼ cup (60 ml) butter over medium-high heat in a 3-quart (3 l) sauté pan. Add the shallot and sauté 2 to 3 minutes until translucent. Add the mushrooms and sauté for 10 minutes, seasoning with salt and white pepper.

Over low heat, mash the potatoes with potato masher. Add the sautéed mushrooms, half-and-half, and remaining ¼ cup (60 ml) butter to the potatoes and stir to combine. Finish with salt and pepper to taste. Serve hot.

Spaghetti with Baby Artichokes and Dandelion Greens
Serves 2

¼ cup (60 ml) plus 2 tablespoons (30 ml) fresh lemon juice
10 baby artichokes, trimmed
6 ounces (170 g) spaghetti
½ cup (125 ml) extra virgin olive oil, plus more as needed
1 salt-packed anchovy fillet, rinsed and chopped
½ teaspoon (2 ml) finely chopped jalapeño
2 cups (500 ml) dandelion greens, chopped
2 cloves garlic, finely chopped
1 teaspoon (5 ml) grated lemon zest
Salt and pepper

Fill a pot with 2 quarts (2 l) water and ¼ cup (60 ml) lemon juice and bring to a boil. Add the artichokes and boil for 10 minutes, or until tender. Drain. Cut into halves. Add the cooked artichokes to 1 quart (1 l) cold water and 2 tablespoon (30 ml) lemon juice. Chill.

Bring a large pot of salted water to a boil. Add the spaghetti and cook until al dente, according to the package directions. Drain well.

Drain the artichokes. Heat the oil in a 10-inch (25 cm) sauté pan over medium heat. Add the anchovy, breaking it up as it cooks. Sauté for 5 seconds. Add the jalapeño and sauté for 15 seconds. Add the dandelion greens and garlic and sauté until the greens are just tender, 2 minutes. Be careful not to burn the garlic. Add the lemon zest and season with salt and pepper.

Add the artichokes and dandelion green mixture to the pasta and toss lightly. Drizzle with more olive oil as desired and serve.

Chef Schenten's Venison and Beef Pot Pie
Serves 8 to 10

The pie crust can be made several days ahead. This recipe requires two batches; It's much more manageable if the first batch is made separately from the second batch. When making pie crust, all ingredients and the food-processor bowl and blade should be well chilled.

MEAT AND MARINADE:
3 cups (750 ml) dry red wine
2 cups (500 ml) beef stock or broth
¼ cup (60 ml) brandy
1 large onion, chopped
2 small carrots, chopped
4 garlic cloves, sliced

1½ pounds (675 g) beef chuck, cut into 2-inch (5 cm) cubes
1½ pounds (675 g) venison, cut into 2-inch (5 cm) cubes

1 teaspoon (5 ml) dried thyme
1 teaspoon (5 ml) dried rosemary
10 peppercorns
12 parsley stems
4 whole cloves
4 allspice berries
1 bay leaf

Salt and pepper
All-purpose flour

8 ounces (225 g) slab bacon (rind removed and set aside)

1 tablespoon (15 ml) vegetable oil
1 tablespoon (15 ml) tomato paste

1 pound (450 g) pearl onions
9 tablespoons (135 ml) butter, at room temperature, divided
Pinch of sugar
Water

1 pound (450 g) button mushrooms
2 cups (500 ml) chopped carrots
1 cup (250 ml) frozen peas

PIE CRUST:
2½ cups (625 ml) all-purpose flour
¼ teaspoon (1 ml) salt
1 cup (250 ml) unsalted butter
¼ cup (60 ml) ice water

To make the marinade, in a large glass baking dish or zippered plastic bag, combine the wine, beef stock, brandy, onion, carrots, and garlic. Add the beef and venison.

Combine the thyme, rosemary, peppercorns, parsley stems, cloves, allspice berries, and bay leaf and put into a mesh teabag or cheesecloth pouch. Add to the meat mixture.

Refrigerate for at least 12 hours.

Strain the meat, reserving the marinade. Separate the vegetables and set aside. With a paper towel, pat the meat dry, season with salt and pepper, and dust lightly with flour.

Preheat the oven to 275°F (135°C).
Slice the bacon slab into 1x¼-inch (2.5 cm x 6 mm) thick strips. Heat the oil over medium-high heat in a large Dutch oven. Add bacon pieces and cook until crispy. Remove the bacon with a slotted spoon and set aside.

Return the Dutch oven to high heat. Add the beef and brown all sides. Transfer to paper toweling. Next, brown venison quickly (as it has a low fat content) on all sides. Transfer to paper towels.

Combine the marinated vegetables, tomato paste, and oil in a large Dutch oven and cook for 5 minutes over medium heat. Add marinade liquid, meat, and bagged herb mix to the pan and bring to a simmer.

Bake for 2 hours. When meat is tender, strain the solids. Return the meat to the pot full of liquid; add bacon pieces.

In large skillet, combine the onions, 2 tablespoons (30 ml) butter, and sugar. Add water to cover. Season with salt and pepper to taste. Simmer the onions until slightly tender. Turn the heat to high and boil to reduce the liquid until the onions become caramelized. Add the onions to stew.

In the same skillet, melt 4 tablespoons (60 ml) of the butter over medium-high heat. Add mushrooms and salt and pepper to taste. Sauté until nicely browned. Add the mushrooms to stew. Add the carrots and peas.

Mix 3 tablespoons (45 ml) butter and 3 tablespoons (50 ml) flour with a fork to form into pea-sized pellets (often referred to as *beurre manie*). Bring the stew to a simmer. Gradually add as many pellets as needed to thicken. Stir.

To make the pie crust, combine the flour and salt in the bowl of a food processor fitted with a chopping blade and pulse until combined. Cut each stick of butter into 32 cubes by splitting the stick lengthwise, and each half lengthwise again, then divide each into 8 cubes.

Place in the food processor. Pulse with the flour mixture until it resembles a coarse meal with lumps. Turn on food processor and add water through the pouring shoot until the dough holds together in a ball. Be careful not to overwork the pastry, as it will result in a tough, not tender, crust. The amount of water needed may vary with each batch. The dough should stick together when pinched. Refrigerate for up to several days.

Preheat the oven to 450°F (230°C).

Lay the pie crust pastry down on a lightly floured surface. Cut each batch of dough in half; form each into a disk. Wrap three pieces in plastic wrap and keep refrigerated until you are ready to use it. Roll out a disk to form a 14-inch (35.5 cm) circle, about 1/16-inch (1.5 mm) thick. Take 1 piece and carefully place into bottom of a tart pan; press gently along the bottom and sides of the pan. Fill to just below the top with stew. Roll out a second piece of pastry, lay over the top of the stew, and crimp around the perimeter to seal the two layers together. Poke the top of the pastry once or twice with fork to allow steam to vent while the pie is in the oven. Repeat with the remaining pastry and stew.

Place the pies on baking sheets. Bake for about 1 hour, until tops are golden brown. Serve immediately out of the oven, or wait 10 minutes and serve hot.

Wild Rice Cakes
Serves 4 to 6

1/2 cup (120 ml) plus 3 tablespoons (45 ml) butter, divided
2 tablespoons (30 ml) diced onion
2 tablespoons (30 ml) diced red bell pepper
2 tablespoons (30 ml) diced yellow bell pepper
1 tablespoon (15 ml) dried chipotle pepper
1 tablespoon (15 ml) minced garlic
1/2 cup (120 ml) crumbs
1/4 cup (60 ml) whipping cream
1 cup (250 ml) cooked wild rice
Salt and pepper
2/3 cup (150 ml) vegetable stock or broth
Sour cream, to garnish

Wash rice thoroughly. In a heavy saucepan, add the rice to the vegetable stock and salt to taste. Bring to a boil. Stir, reduce heat to simmer, cover and cook 40 to 45 minutes until kernels puff open. Uncover and fluff with fork. Set aside.

Melt 1/2 cup (120 ml) of the butter in saucepan over medium heat. Add the onion, red and yellow peppers, chipotle, and garlic. Sauté until soft but not browned, about 5 minutes. Remove from the heat and fold in the crumbs, whipping cream, and cooked rice. Season with salt and pepper. Form into small cakes 3 to 4 inches (7.5 to 10 cm) in diameter.

Melt the remaining 3 tablespoons (50 ml) butter in a large skillet over medium to high heat. Fry until crisp, about 2 minutes per side. Depending on the size of your skillet, you may have to fry in batches. Drain on paper towels.

Serve hot, garnished with sour cream.

Pasta, Peas, and Pesto
Serves 4

Arugula, an aromatic herb with a touch of bitter, peppery, mustard flavor, is a novel ingredient for a unique pesto.

PESTO:
1/2 cup (125 ml) chopped arugula leaves
1/2 cup (125 ml) fresh basil leaves
5 cloves garlic
3 tablespoons (50 ml) pine nuts
1/4 cup (60 ml) extra virgin olive oil

FLAVORED OIL:
1 cup (250 ml) extra virgin olive oil
5 to 6 cloves garlic, chopped
1 shallot, chopped

PASTA:
1 1/2 cups (375 ml) fresh peas (or substitute chopped asparagus or broccoli florets)
1 pound (450 g) pasta shells or similar-size pasta
Salt, freshly ground black pepper, and crushed red pepper flakes
2 cups (500 ml) grated fresh Romano cheese
Toasted pine nuts or chopped sun-dried tomatoes and scallions, to garnish

To make the pesto, combine the arugula with the basil in a food processor. Add the garlic and pine nuts. Pulse for 15 to 20 seconds at a time while slowly adding olive oil. Set aside.

To make the flavored oil, bring the olive oil to a simmer in a small saucepan. Add the garlic and simmer for 5 minutes over low heat. Add the shallot and simmer for 2 more minutes. Pour the oil through strainer and reserve.

Steam the peas for approximately 5 minutes until tender crisp.

Cook the pasta in a large pot of boiling salted water until al dente. Drain. Do not rinse pasta. Transfer to a serving dish, add the pesto, 2 tablespoons (30 ml) at a time, and toss gently. Add the cheese and toss gently. Add 1/3 cup (75 ml) of the flavored oil and the peas. Toss gently. Add a light sprinkle of salt, black pepper, and red pepper to taste.

Garnish with grated Romano cheese, toasted pine nuts or sun-dried tomatoes and scallions and serve immediately.

Wild Rice and Chicken-of-the-Woods Mushrooms

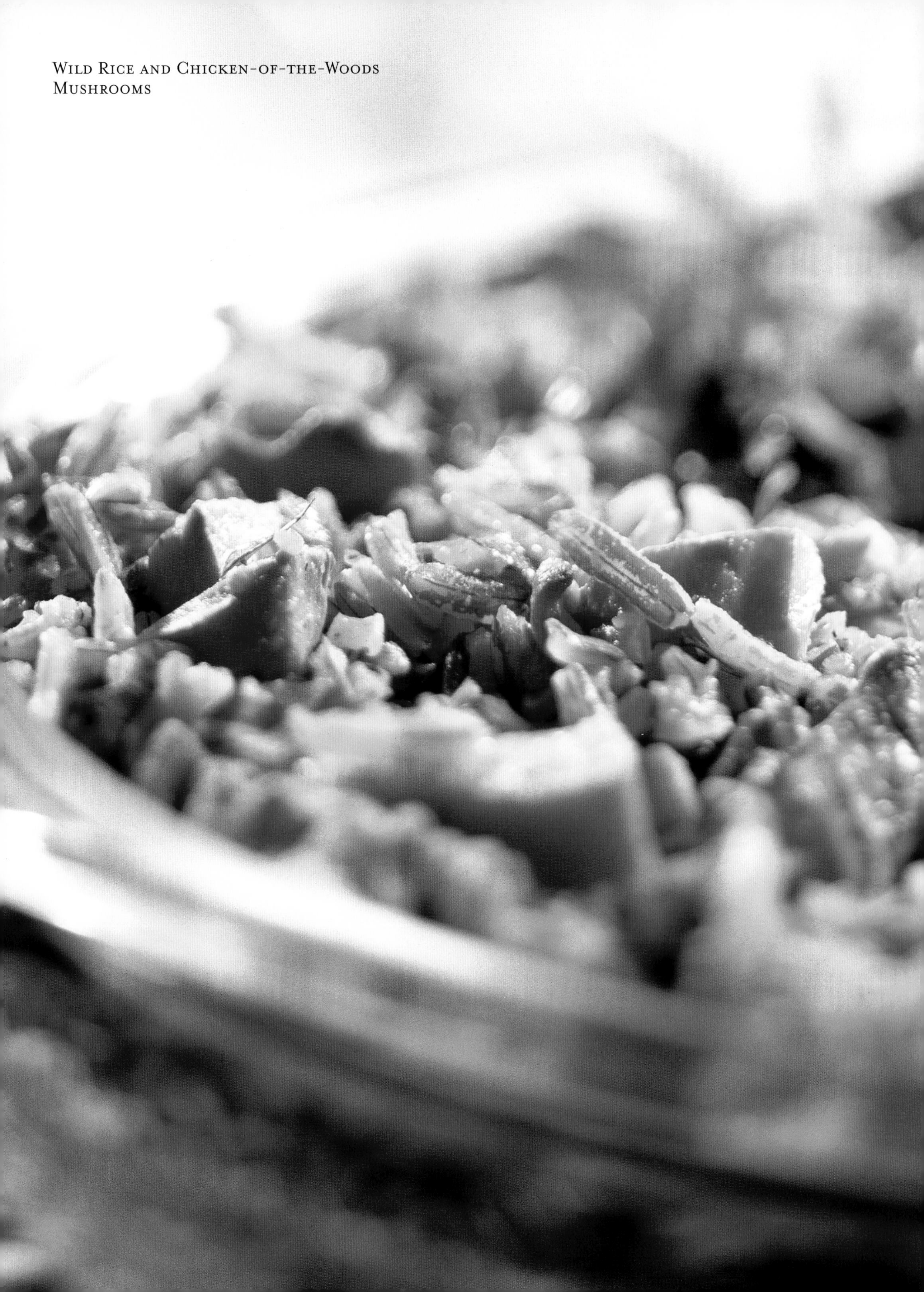

Wild Rice and Chicken-of-the-Woods Mushrooms

Serves 12

4 tablespoons (60 ml) butter, divided
2 shallots, finely minced
2 cups (500 ml) chicken-of-the-woods mushrooms, cleaned and diced
2 tablespoons (30 ml) white wine or sherry (optional, but recommended)
1 cup (250 ml) wild rice
4 cups (1 l) chicken stock or broth
Salt and pepper
¼ cup (60 ml) flat-leaf parsley, finely minced

In a 5-quart (5 l) saucepan, melt 2 tablespoons (30 ml) of the butter over medium-high heat. Add the shallots and briefly sauté until translucent. Add the mushrooms and sauté for 10 minutes. Add the wine, if using, and sauté another 10 minutes.

In a 4-quart (4 l) saucepan, melt the remaining 2 tablespoons (30 ml) butter over medium heat. Add the wild rice and sauté for 5 minutes. Combine with mushroom mixture and chicken stock. Add salt and pepper to taste. Cover and bring to boil over high heat. Reduce the heat to low and simmer for 20 minutes. Uncover, fluff the rice, add parsley, and, if necessary, continue heating on low to evaporate any remaining liquid.

Serve hot.

Wild Rice Mélange

Serves 8

3 tablespoons (50 ml) butter or olive oil
½ cup (125 ml) chopped onion
8 to 12 medium brussels sprouts, cored and separated into leaves
1 cup (250 ml) cooked wild rice
½ cup (125 ml) cooked orzo
⅓ cup (75 ml) pepitas (unsalted, hulled, green pumpkin seeds), toasted
Sea salt and freshly ground black pepper

In a large skillet, melt the butter over medium-high heat. Add onion and sauté until tender, about 3 minutes. Stir in brussels sprout leaves and sauté for 3 minutes. Stir in the wild rice, orzo, and pepitas. Reduce the heat to medium and cook, stirring, until the mixture is hot, about 5 minutes. Season to taste with salt and pepper.

Serve hot.

Chicken-of-the-Woods Mushrooms

This spectacular wild bracket fungus grows on tree stumps, often on sweet chestnut, oak, and beech. It grows into fleshy, knobby clusters with shell or feather-like curves. The largest ever found weighed 100 pounds.

This suede-looking two-toned mass is unmistakable with its orange top and a sulfur-yellow underneath.

When the mushroom is young, its thick flesh is solid and smoothly uniform, breaking into fiberless golden chunks. Only the edges of new growth, however, are tender enough to eat, having a tasty hint of lemony chicken.

Tip: These mushrooms become dry and crumbly when they are too old to eat.

Spinach Pierogi

Makes 16 pierogis (enough for 4 appetizers or 2 entrées)

This is the kind of dish that cries the verdant whelps of spring in a hallelujah chorus that will make you smile with every bite. If you do not have fiddleheads, asparagus would work well as a substitute. You can freeze pierogis before they are boiled and use them later. Spread them out on a tray so they don't touch, then transfer them to a heavy-duty zippered bag when they are fully frozen. They should keep for 3 months. To cook them, do not thaw, simply put them frozen into the boiling water and proceed as directed in the recipe.

DOUGH:
2 large russet potatoes (about 1 pound/450 g each)
2 cups (500 ml) all-purpose flour, plus more for dusting
2 medium eggs, at room temperature
Salt and pepper

FILLING:
1 cup (250 ml) whole milk ricotta cheese, well
1/4 cup (60 ml) freshly grated Parmesan cheese, divided
1 bunch spinach, trimmed

1 medium egg
1 tablespoon (15 ml) grated lemon zest
Pinch of nutmeg
Salt and pepper

BROWN BUTTER:
1 cup (220 g) butter

VEGETABLES:
4 ounces (225 g) fiddlehead ferns (ostrich fern coils)
1 carrot, finely diced
1 rib celery, finely diced
1 onion, finely diced
1/2 cup (125 ml) fresh or frozen peas
1 bunch spinach, trimmed

BLASAMIC REDUCTION:
2 cups (500 ml) balsamic vinegar
1 cup (250 ml) good-quality red wine
1/4 cup (60 ml) honey

SAUCE:
1 small shallot, finely chopped
¼ teaspoon capers (1 ml), rinsed
Pinch of crushed red pepper flakes
1 tablespoon (15 ml) whole butter
2 to 4 tablespoons (30 to 60 ml) chicken stock

WALNUT GARNISH:
½ cup (125 ml) walnuts, toasted
Olive oil
Salt
Cayenne pepper

Preheat the oven to 350° F (180°C).

Bake the potatoes for 1½ hours or until they are very crusty on the outside. Remove and, when cool enough to handle, peel and run them through a ricer in a large mixing bowl. Set them aside to cool at room temperature. (Do not refrigerate; the potatoes will absorb moisture and make the pierogis gooey.)

Fill a large bowl with ice and water to shock the vegetables in when you are done blanching them.

Blanch the carrot, celery and onion. Transfer to the ice water with a slotted spoon.

Blanch the peas (if they are fresh). Transfer to the ice water with a slotted spoon.

Blanch spinach for the filling. Transfer to the ice water with tongs.

Remove the blanched vegetables from the ice water and set aside in a large bowl.

Blanch the ferns for 30 seconds, then shock in the ice water. Repeat this for a total of 3 times. This is to remove any impurities and the papery covering if present.

Make brown butter by simmering the butter over medium heat until it gets foamy and begins to brown and smell nutty. Remove immediately and transfer to a cool, dry container. Scrape any of the browned solids that may have collected on the bottom of the pan into the butter as well. Reserve.

To make the balsamic reduction, reduce the vinegar, wine, and honey in a small pan over medium heat at a slow simmer until it can coat the back of a spoon. It should reduce to about 1 cup (250 ml). Strain and reserve.

Make the filling by combining the cheeses, spinach and egg. Season with nutmeg, lemon zest, salt, and pepper.

To make the dough, form a well in the riced potatoes and crack one egg into the center. Sprinkle lightly with flour and season with salt and pepper. Begin by mixing the egg with a

fork and then with your hands to incorporate the potatoes. Add the rest of the flour and use a smearing motion with the palm of you hands to fully incorporate the flour into the dough. The dough should be slightly springy when you touch it with your fingers. Dust lightly with flour and cover with a dry towel.

On a slightly dusted surface, roll out a small portion of the dough with a floured rolling pin to about ¼ inch (5 mm) thickness. Cut into circles with a pastry ring (biscuit cutter). Put about 1 teaspoon (5 ml) of filling into the center of each dough circle and bring the sides together to form half-moons or purses and lightly pinch to seal. Repeat until all the dough and filling is used.

Bring a large pot of salted water (3 tablespoons per gallon/ 50 ml per 3.75 l) to a light boil. Set up an ice-water bath near the boiling water. Drop the pierogis, a few at a time, into the boiling water and when they float, 4 to 5 minutes, carefully remove them and transfer to the ice bath. Repeat until all the pierogi are cooked.

When cool, toss the pierogis with a bit of olive oil so they do not stick together. Refrigerate in a sealed container until you are ready to use them.

To serve, melt enough brown butter over medium-high heat to cover the bottom of the pan about ¼ inch (5 cm) deep. Fry the pierogis about 3 minutes on each side until browned. Drain on a paper towel.

Make a sauce with 1 tablespoon (15 ml) of the balsamic reduction, chichen stock, capers, shallots, and whole butter.

Melt a little butter in a saucepan over medium heat. Add the the blanched peas, fiddleheads, carrot, celery, and onion. Stir in the spinach and cook until wilted.

Spoon the vegetables on a plate and top with the pierogis. Pour the sauce over the top and then sprinkle a little Parmesan and the walnuts to garnish.

Wild Rice

Perhaps thousands of years ago, wild rice was discovered growing in the cool, clear lakes of Minnesota, Wisconsin, Michigan, and Canada.

As native Americans moved westward into wild rice areas, one thing was quickly discovered: survival was contingent upon this resilient and indigenous food.

Wild rice, technically an aquatic grass seed, is found on the vast shallow flats and marshes of lakes, slow-moving rivers, and streams. As the winter ice melts away it begins sprouting in early spring. Eventually the stalks rise a few feet above the water's surface, and in late summer they mature and are ready to harvest.

Hand harvesting is a tradition many families still practice today. The rice stalks are drawn into a canoe and "knocked" to free the kernels from the plants. The kernels are then "parched" to remove moisture from inside the seeds. "Jigging" or threshing loosens the hull, and "winnowing" blows away the chaff. Once clean from debris, the rice is ready, or "finished."

Wild Rice Sauté
Serves 6

⅔ cup (150 ml) wild rice
3 tablespoons (45 ml) butter
¼ small red onion, finely diced
2 tablespoons (30 ml) minced fresh parsley (optional)
1 cup (250 ml) thinly sliced peeled root vegetables (rutabaga, turnip, carrot, celery root, parsnip)
½ pound (225 g) mushrooms, trimmed
½ teaspoon (2 ml) ground cinnamon
1 teaspoon (5 ml) kosher salt or coarse sea salt
½ to 1 teaspoon (2 to 5 ml) black pepper
2 to 4 tablespoons (30 to 60 ml) chopped walnuts, pecans, or hazelnuts (optional)
¼ cup (60 ml) water

Combine the rice with 10 cups (2.5 l) water in a saucepan, bring to a boil, and boil until rice is tender, about 15 minutes. When the wild rice is done to your liking, drain well and spread out to cool. Depending on the specific type of wild rice and the doneness you like, you should have 2 to 2½ cups (500 to 625 ml) cooked wild rice.

In a large heavy sauté pan or wok, melt the butter over medium heat. When the butter is foamy, add the onion and the root vegetables. Toss well a couple of times and sauté for about 2 minutes. Add the mushrooms, cinnamon, salt, and pepper and toss well. Cook for about 1 minute. Add the cooked rice, parsley and nuts, if using, and toss well. Cook for about 3 minutes, stirring or tossing occasionally. Add the water. This will immediately create steam. Toss once and let cook until the steam subsides, about 1 minute. Toss again and serve.

Potato Galette with Chive Sour Cream
Serves 4

¼ cup (60 ml) sour cream
2 tablespoons (30 ml) finely chopped onion
1 tablespoon (15 ml) snipped fresh chives
2 teaspoons (10 ml) lemon juice
3 medium russet potatoes, peeled and grated (2½ cups/625 ml)
4 tablespoons (60 ml) butter, melted, divided
Salt and pepper to taste

In small bowl, combine sour cream, onion, chives and juice. Set aside.

Preheat oven to 400°F (200°C). In medium mixing bowl, combine potatoes and 2 tablespoons (30 ml) butter. Toss to coat. Stir in salt and pepper. Heat 10-inch (25 cm) ovenproof skillet over high heat. Add remaining 2 tablespoons (30 ml) butter to skillet and swirl to coat. Add potatoes to skillet, pressing to flatten potatoes into one pancake.

Cook over high heat for 2 minutes. Reduce heat to medium. Cook for 2 to 4 minutes longer, or until bottom of galette is golden brown. Turn galette over by inverting onto a plate, then sliding it back into skillet. Cook for 4 to 5 minutes, or until second side is golden brown.

Place skillet in oven. Bake galette for 12 to 15 minutes, or until crisp. Serve galette with chive sour cream.

Soups and Stews

What is it about soups and stews?
There seems to be a special place in
everyone's heart for these wonderful
"comfort" foods. From childhood we
remember the mesmerizing effect a
simple bowl had on us—waving our
spoon methodically back and forth and
discovering some delectable tidbit
of vegetable or meat.

Even today, soups and stews warm
our bodies as well as our spirits.
Especially so, when the ingredients
are drawn from nature.

Autumn Squash Soup

Serves 8 to 12

2 sweet potatoes, peeled and chopped
1 butternut squash, peeled, seeded, and chopped
1 acorn squash, peeled, seeded, and chopped
2 carrots, chopped
2 tablespoons (30 ml) olive oil
1 medium onion, chopped
2 ribs celery, chopped
1 leek, chopped white and green parts
2 apples, cored, peeled, and chopped
4 cloves garlic
1 cup (250 ml) apple cider
6 cups (1.5 l) vegetable stock or broth
2 tablespoons (30 ml) honey
2 teaspoons (10 ml) jerk seasoning
1 cup (250 ml) heavy cream

Preheat the oven to 350°F (180°C).

Season and roast the sweet potatoes and squash in oven for 50 to 60 minutes, until golden brown. Set aside.

Sauté carrots in oil in a large skillet over medium heat for 6 to 8 minutes. Add the onion, celery, leek, apples, and garlic and sauté for 5 minutes or until tender and onions and garlic are translucent. Add the cider and simmer until the liquid is reduced by half. Add the stock, honey, jerk seasoning, roasted squash and sweet potatoes and simmer for 30 minutes.

Purée the soup in a food processor or blender until smooth, working in small batches if necessary. Let cool slightly so steam doesn't blow the lid off.

Return the soup to the pan, add the cream, and heat through. Serve hot.

Creamy Potato and Mustard Soup

Serves 8

2 tablespoons (30 ml) butter
1 medium leek, white part only, thinly sliced
4 cloves garlic, crushed
6 medium German yellow or Yukon Gold potatoes, peeled and sliced
6 cups (1.5 l) chicken stock or broth
3 cups (750 ml) whipping cream
¼ to ½ cup (60 to 125 ml) Dijon mustard
Sea salt and freshly ground white pepper
Croutons, to garnish
Sliced chives or scallions, to garnish

In large saucepan, melt the butter over medium heat. Add the leek and sauté for 5 minutes, stirring occasionally. Add the garlic and sauté until tender, about 5 minutes.

Add the potatoes and chicken stock; heat to boiling. Reduce the heat and simmer, covered, until potatoes are very tender, about 10 minutes.

Using an immersion blender, purée the soup. (The soup may also be puréed in batches in a regular blender and returned to the saucepan.) Add the cream and heat until hot. Stir in mustard and season to taste with salt and pepper.

Serve hot, garnishing each serving with croutons and chives.

Forest Mushroom and Fennel Soup

Serves 6 to 8

To make a truly delicious soup, lightly season every stage of the soup with salt for a better and more complex end result. If you like, save the fennel fronds (green tops) for a garnish. You can substitute dill for the tarragon, and garnish with sour cream.

2 pounds (900 g) button mushrooms, chopped
Salt
3 quarts (3 l) chicken stock or broth or water
Canola oil
1 pound (450 g) fresh seasonal mixed mushrooms; washed and quartered or sliced
1 bulb fennel, diced
¼ cup (60 ml) butter
1 large leek, diced, white and tender green parts
2 cloves garlic, minced
1 cup (250 ml) white wine or dry sherry
1 very small bunch fresh tarragon, chopped
Black pepper

To make the mushroom stock, in a stock pot, lightly salt the crushed button mushrooms and add chicken stock. Bring to a boil, reduce the heat, and simmer for 15 minutes Strain into a large bowl, pressing hard on the solids to extract as much liquid as possible. Set aside. Dice and reserve mushrooms.

To make the soup, heat 2 tablespoons (30 ml) of the canola oil in a stock pot over high heat. Add the mixed mushrooms and sauté until well browned, about 15 minutes. Remove the mushrooms from the pot with a slotted spoon. Add more oil, if needed. Add the fennel and sauté until caramelized, 15 minutes. Remove and set aside. Lower the heat and add the butter, leek, and garlic. Sweat gently for 5 minutes. Add the wine and reduce until it is almost gone.

Return all the sautéed ingredients back to pot. Add the chopped button mushrooms and mushroom stock. Simmer for 10 minutes. Add the tarragon and salt and pepper to taste.

Serve hot in soup bowls.

Soup Stock

A truly satisfying soup always starts with a good-quality stock—vegetable, beef, veal, poultry, fish, or seafood.

Whatever recipe you're making, it pays to set aside your carcasses from such prizes as free-range chicken, wild turkey, duck, and upland game birds. Later you can put them into zippered plastic bags, label, and freeze until you have enough stored up for a nice batch of stock.

The stock you make can, of course, be used right away to make soup, or frozen for later use. It's like liquid gold for sauces, soups, stews, and risotto.

Lake Trout Chowder
Serves 4 to 6

4 cups (6 medium) red potatoes, peeled and cut into ½-inch (1.3 cm) cubes
Water
2 teaspoons (10 ml) salt
15 whole peppercorns
6 allspice berries
½ cup (120 ml) margarine or butter
1 can (12 ounces/354 ml) evaporated milk
2 medium onions, thinly sliced
2 pounds (900 g) lake trout or other freshwater fillets (8 ounces/225 g each), skin removed and cut into 2-inch (5 cm) pieces
3 tablespoons (50 ml) snipped fresh parsley

Put the potatoes in a 4-quart (4 l) Dutch oven or stockpot. Add just enough water to cover the potatoes. Bring to a boil over medium-high heat. Add the salt, peppercorns, and allspice. Cook for 3 to 5 minutes, or until potatoes are tender crisp. Reduce the heat to medium-low. Add the margarine and evaporated milk. Stir until the margarine is melted.

Layer the onion slices over the potatoes. Arrange the trout pieces on top of the onions. Simmer (do not boil) for 20 to 30 minutes, or until fish is firm and opaque and just begins to flake and onions are tender, turning the trout pieces over once or twice.

Serve hot, sprinkling each serving evenly with parsley.

Wild Leek Soup
Serves 4 to 6

2 tablespoons (30 ml) butter
1 small yellow onion, finely sliced
2 garlic cloves, chopped
2 dozen wild leeks (white and green parts), chopped (or substitute scallions)
4 medium potatoes, peeled and chopped
2 cups (500 ml) chicken stock or broth
1 quart (1 l) chicken stock or broth
Salt and pepper
3 ounces (100 ml) cream (or scant ⅓ to ½ cup/75 to 125 ml)

GARNISH:
Hazelnut oil
Fresh ground nutmeg

Melt the butter in a saucepan over low heat. Add leeks and onion and sauté for 5 minutes. Add garlic and sauté for 2 more minutes or until softened. Add potatoes to pan and heat for 3 additional minutes, then add enough stock to cover the onions and potatoes. Cook until both are soft, 12 to 14 minutes.

Strain the vegetables, reserving the cooking stock. Purée the vegetables in a blender or food processor, adding stock as needed.

Return the purée to the saucepan and heat through. Season with salt and pepper and whisk in cream. Add the remaining stock as needed to achieve the desired consistency and whisk until smooth.

To serve, ladle the soup into bowls, drizzle with hazelnut oil, and sprinkle with nutmeg.

Rabbit Soup with Dumplings

Serves 4

SOUP:
4 tablespoons (60 ml) olive oil, divided
1 large onion, diced, divided
4 large carrots, diced
4 ribs celery, diced
1 rabbit (1½ to 2 pounds/675 to 900 g), skinned, rinsed, quartered, and boneless meat cut into small pieces
6 cups (1.5 l) chicken stock or broth or water
1 cup (250 ml) wild rice, rinsed well

DUMPLINGS:
2 cups (500 ml) all-purpose flour
1 tablespoon (15 ml) baking soda
1 teaspoon (5 ml) salt
1 cup (250 ml) whole milk
3 tablespoons (45 g) unsalted butter, melted

To make the soup, in a large skillet, heat 2 tablespoons (30 ml) of the oil over medium heat. Add half the onion and cook until lightly browned, 5 minutes. Add the carrots and sauté for about 5 minutes. Add the celery and sauté for 5 more minutes. Remove with a slotted spoon and set aside.

Heat the remaining 2 tablespoons (30 ml) oil in the skillet. Add the rabbit pieces and other half of onion. Sauté for 3 to 5 minutes and turn the pieces, so both sides are browned. Set aside.

Pour the stock and wild rice into a 4-quart (4-l) saucepan. Bring to a boil. Let simmer on medium heat for about 20 minutes. (Cooking times for wild rice can range widely because of how the rice was processed and the size of the grain.) Add reserved cooked vegetables and rabbit. Stir well.

To make the dumplings, mix together the flour, baking soda, and salt in a large bowl. Add the milk and melted butter. Use a pastry knife, fork, or your hands to mix until it just begins to combine. Overmixing can cause tough dumplings. Form the dough into 15 to 20 balls.

Add the dumplings to the soup, cover, and simmer for 8 to 10 minutes. To test to see that the dumplings are fully cooked, insert a toothpick; it should come out clean when the dumpling is done. So test it a few times during cooking. Rice is done when fluffed up and some of the inner white part is exposed.

Serve hot.

Wild Game Rendang

Serves 6

This Malaysian recipe is a stunning way to honor the meat of any special large game animal. The rich, perfumy blend of spices dominates the dish no matter what meat is used. In Malaysian cuisine, the spices are often paired with lamb. The long cooking time in this tenderizing blend makes even the toughest cuts palatable. Most ingredients are found in Southeast Asian markets, with the galangal and kaffir lime leaves the hardest find outside of the supermarket. Serve with basmati rice and a simple seasoned rice-vinegar salad.

CHILE PASTE:
1 cup (250 ml) coarsely chopped shallots
2 cloves garlic
2 small Thai chiles, stemmed and seeded
2 tablespoons (30 ml) grated fresh or frozen coconut (or substitute 1 tablespoon/15 ml dried unsweetened coconut)

RENDANG:
1 pound (450 g) game meat for stewing, cut into 2-inch chunks
2¼ cups (560 ml) fresh coconut milk or 1 (18.5-ounce/510 g) can
1 stalk lemongrass, dried outer leaf discarded, lower pale stalk trimmed of upper green portion, and crushed
1½-inch (3.8 cm) piece galangal (golf-ball size), crushed
2 kaffir lime leaves
1 tablespoon (15 ml) coriander seeds
½ teaspoon (2 ml) cumin seeds
¼ teaspoon (1 ml) ground turmeric
¼ cup (60 ml) brown sugar
1 large or 2 small sweet potatoes, peeled and cut into 2-inch (5 cm) pieces
2 Yukon Gold potatoes, peeled and cut into 2-inch (5 cm) pieces
3 large carrots, cut into 2-inch (5 cm) pieces
2 onions, cut into 2-inch (5 cm) wedges
½ cup (125 ml) beef stock or broth (optional)

To make the chile paste, combine the shallots, garlic, chiles, and coconut in a large mortar and pestle or a food processor and grind. Thoroughly coat the game chunks with chile paste. Marinate for 1 hour.

In a large nonstick saucepan, sear the game until browned on all sides, 2 to 3 minutes. Add the coconut milk, lemongrass, galangal, lime leaves, coriander seeds, cumin seeds, turmeric, and brown sugar. Bring to a boil over medium-high heat. Turn down the heat and simmer for 1 hour, uncovered.

Add the sweet potatoes, white potatoes, carrots, and onions. Add the beef stock if not enough liquid remains to steam them. Cover and simmer for 25 minutes until the vegetables are tender. Serve hot.

Cajun Seafood Gumbo

Serves 6

SEASONING MIX:
2 whole bay leaves
2 teaspoons (10 ml) salt
½ teaspoon (2 ml) black pepper
½ teaspoon (2 ml) red pepper (preferable cayenne)
½ teaspoon (2 ml) white pepper
½ teaspoon (2 ml) dried thyme leaves
¼ teaspoon (1 ml) dried oregano leaves

GUMBO:
2 cups (500 ml) chopped onion
1½ cups (375 ml) chopped green bell peppers
1 cup (250 ml) chopped celery
¾ cup (175 ml) vegetable oil
¾ cup (175 ml) all-purpose flour
1 tablespoon (15 ml) minced garlic
5½ cups (1.4 l) chicken stock or broth
1 pound (450 g) andouille or other smoked sausage,
    cut into ½ inch (1.3 cm) pieces
1 pound (450 g) medium shrimp, peeled
¾ pound (330 g) crabmeat
2½ cups (625 ml) hot cooked rice
Chopped scallion, to garnish

To make the seasoning mix, in a small bowl, combine the bay leaves, salt, black pepper, red pepper, white pepper, thyme, and oregano. Mix well and set aside.

Combine the onions, bell peppers, and celery in a medium-size bowl and set aside.

Heat the oil in a large heavy skillet over high heat until it begins to smoke, about 5 minutes. Gradually add the flour, whisking constantly with a long-handled metal whisk. Continue cooking over medium-low heat, whisking constantly, until roux is red-brown, 5 to 6 minutes, being careful not to let it scorch or splash on your skin. Immediately add half the vegetables and cook and stir for about 2 minutes. Stir in the seasoning mix and continue cooking for about 2 minutes, stirring frequently. Add the garlic; stir well, then cook and stir for about 1 minute more. Remove from the heat.

Meanwhile, pour the stock into a 6-quart (5 l) saucepan or large Dutch oven. Bring to a boil. Add the roux mixture by spoonfuls to the boiling stock, stirring until dissolved between each addition. Bring the mixture to a boil. Add the andouille sausage and return to a boil; continue boiling for 15 minutes, stirring occasionally. Reduce the heat and simmer for 10 minutes more. Add the shrimp and crabmeat, stir occasionally, and skim any oil from the surface.

Serve steaming hot in a large soup bowl, over rice and garnished with chopped scallion.

Catfish Gumbo

Serves 6

½ cup (125 ml) chopped celery
½ cup (125 ml) chopped onion
1 garlic clove, minced
½ cup (125 ml) chopped green pepper
¼ cup (60 ml) vegetable oil
4 cups (1 l) beef broth
1 can (14.5-ounce/411 grams) peeled tomatoes
1 package (10-ounce/284 grams) frozen, sliced okra
2 teaspoons (10 ml) salt
1 teaspoon (5 ml) black pepper
¼ teaspoon (1 ml) thyme
1 bay leaf
Dash of Louisiana hot sauce
1 pound (450 g) catfish fillets
1½ cups (375 ml) hot cooked rice

Cook celery, onion, garlic and green pepper in oil until tender. Add broth, tomatoes, okra and seasonings. Cover and simmer for 30 minutes. Cut catfish into 1-inch (2.5 cm) pieces, and add to simmering mixture. Cover and simmer 15 minutes longer or until fish flakes easily. Remove bay leaf. Place ¼ cup (60 ml) rice in each bowl. Fill with gumbo and serve.

Garden Gazpacho Soup

Serves 4 to 6

Serve with crusty bread and artisan cheese for a cooling lunch.

1 cucumber, peeled, seeded, and diced
1 Vidalia or other sweet onion, minced
2 cloves garlic, minced
3 large tomatoes, peeled, seeded, and diced
1 green bell pepper, diced
1 orange bell pepper, diced
2 cups (500 ml) tomato juice
1½ cups (375 ml) chicken stock or broth
¼ cup (60 ml) fresh finely chopped parsley
1 teaspoon (5 ml) dried oregano
1 teaspoon (5 ml) dried basil
¼ teaspoon (1 ml) hot pepper sauce
½ teaspoon (2 ml) sea salt
½ teaspoon (2 ml) ground black pepper
¼ cup (60 ml) champagne vinegar

Combine all ingredients in a large bowl; chill for at least 6 hours. You can also purée the mixture in a blender, reserving some of the chopped vegetables for topping. Serve cold.

Entrées

The original North American natives lived and
moved with the seasons, hunting big and
small game, fish and birds throughout the year.
Today, these foods from nature
serve as the centerpiece of a delectable meal,
lending their tastes, textures, and colors.

Early-spring fishing, for instance,
coincides with the growing seasons of
morel mushrooms and fiddlehead ferns—
offering perfectly matched combinations.
The wild berries of summer often
make their way into lovely, flavorful reduction
sauces served with main dishes.
Game birds seem to flock to be paired
with autumn squash and wild rice.
And who can forget the delight of a
winter meal of venison?

Big and Small Game

As the season for harvesting big and small game approaches, a dormant feeling of anticipation begins to stir. To many, it's the romance of hunting and gathering that sparks enthusiasm for the rituals of preparation.

Guns are inspected along with those other familiar items—hunting clothes, backpacks, maps, traps, and rumpled paper with slightly faded strategies—so necessary to the hunt.

Often, the most gratifying part of hunting big and small game is the adventure of preparing ingredients from the wild and sharing them with friends and family.

Venison Chops with Juniper Marinade
Serves 6

MARINADE:
2 tablespoons (30 ml) sunflower oil
¼ cup (60 ml) gin
3 tablespoons (50 ml) pure maple syrup
2 tablespoons (30 ml) coarse salt
1 tablespoon (15 ml) finely minced fresh thyme, or 1 teaspoon (5 ml) dried
3 juniper berries, crushed
2 large garlic cloves, crushed
¼ teaspoon (1 ml) ground cinnamon
⅛ teaspoon (0.5 ml) black pepper

VENISON CHOPS:
12 venison chops, 1 to 1½ inches (2.5 to 3.5 cm) thick, Frenched (flesh removed to expose end of bone), silver skin removed
2 tablespoons (30 ml) sunflower oil, for frying

Combine the marinade ingredients in a gallon-size (3.75 l) heavy-duty zippered plastic bag, add the chops, and refrigerate overnight.

One hour before cooking, remove the bag from the refrigerator to bring the chops to room temperature. Pat the chops dry and discard the marinade.

Preheat the oven to 500°F (260°C).

Heat the oil in a large cast-iron skillet or nonstick pan over medium-high heat until the oil is very hot but not smoking. Fry the chops in batches for 2 minutes on each side. Transfer to a large roasting pan.

Bake the chops for 3 minutes until medium-rare. Remove from the oven, cover loosely with foil, and let stand for 5 minutes before serving.

Spring Lamb or Venison Stew
Serves 6 to 8

Serve with crusty bread.

2 pounds (900 g) lamb or venison stew meat
Salt and pepper
½ cup (125 ml) olive oil
1 pound (450 g) small new potatoes
4 ounces (120 g) sun-dried tomatoes
4 ounces (225 g) sliced ramps (wild leeks), greens separated from bulbs
10 cloves garlic
8 ounces (225 g) morels or mixed wild mushrooms
2 bay leaves
8 cups (2 l) meat or chicken stock or broth
2 cups (500 ml) fresh or frozen peas
1 cup (250 ml) fava beans, shelled and peeled

Season the meat with salt and pepper. Heat the oil in a deep, heavy-bottomed saucepan over medium heat. Add the meat in small batches and brown well, 5 to 8 minutes. Set aside. Sauté the potatoes, tomatoes, ramp bulbs, and whole garlic cloves until brown. Add the morels and cook until soft. Add the bay leaves and stock to just cover ingredients. Simmer, covered, on low for 2 to 3 hours until meat is tender.

Add the peas, fava beans, and ramp greens and adjust the seasoning. Cook long enough to heat through.

Serve hot.

Sausage Making

For as long as I can remember, my grandpa always hunted deer. He never wasted the heart or the liver. The heart was diced up, browned and put with scrambled eggs for lunch. The liver was always fried up with onions, one of my grandma's favorites. Grandpa would grind venison and pork in the kitchen, smoke the meat in the garage, then stuff all of the casings for ring bologna and summer sausage. It took them weeks to get it all done. He was proud of his venison and hunted until the last year of life.

When your prize is brought home, it's a given to prepare the prime tenderloins and chops, but the bulk of the deer remains. With the mind-set of conservation and culinary creativity there is a lot you can do with what is often considered scraps.

Because venison has so little fat, it is often mixed with pork and/or beef in making brats, breakfast links, sausage, cold cuts and jerky. These can be blended with a medly of dried herbs and fruits, wild rice, and even farmstead cheeses. These savory extras are long lasting and freeze beautifully. They are a wonderful way to share your venison with family and friends.

Spicy Venison Sausage with Pancetta
Makes 32 (4-ounce/120 g) or 21 (6-ounce/170 g) sausages

6 pounds (2 3/4 kg) venison meat
2 pounds (900 g) pancetta
¼ cup (60 g) smoked Spanish paprika (pimentón)
2 tablespoons (30 g) crushed red chile flakes
2 tablespoons (30 g) coarsely ground fennel seed
1 cup (250 g) fresh garlic purée
1 cup (250 g) chopped fresh oregano
½ cup (125 g) chopped fresh thyme
⅓ cup (50 g) kosher salt
2 tablespoons (30 g) coarsely ground black pepper
2 cups (500 ml) cold water
6 to 8 feet (1.8 to 2.4 m) natural hog casing packed in salt

Cut the venison and pancetta into appropriate-size pieces to fit through a meat grinder, using a coarse grinding plate. Hand mix the ground meat mixture to evenly distribute the pancetta with the venison. Run through the grinder a second time.

In a large mixing bowl, combine the paprika, chile flakes, fennel seed, garlic purée, oregano, thyme, salt, and pepper. Stir well. Add the cold water and continue to stir until well mixed. Hand mix the meat mixture into spices until evenly distributed.

Fill a sausage stuffer with the bulk meat mix, tapping it down until any air pockets are removed. Hold casing under running water to rinse off salt brine it was packaged in. Feed the casing onto the stuffer and secure the end with a knot. Slowly fill all the casing, twisting the strand of sausage into 6-inch (15 cm) links. Alternate the direction of the twists at every 6-inch (15 cm) interval.

Store the links in a container covered with plastic wrap in the refrigerator for 6 to 12 hours before snipping into individual links. Sausages can be stores in the refrigerator 7 to 10 days, or in the freezer for up to a year if well wrapped.

Fresh-Ground Venison Sausage
Serves 4

1 pound (0.45 kg) lean ground venison, crumbled
1 teaspoon (5 ml) fennel seed
1 teaspoon (5 ml) salt
½ teaspoon (2 ml) garlic powder
¼ to ½ teaspoon (1 to 2 ml) crushed red pepper flakes

In a medium mixing bowl, combine all the ingredients. Mix well. Shape the mixture into eight 3-inch (7.5 cm) patties. In 12-inch (30 cm) nonstick skillet, cook patties over medium heat for 5 to 6 minutes, until the meat is no longer pink in center, turning the patties over once or twice.

The patties can be frozen in sealable plastic bags between layers of wax paper. To prepare from a frozen state, cook the patties in a nonstick skillet over medium-low heat for 18 to 20 minutes, until meat is no longer pink in the center, turning the patties over once or twice.

Serve hot on toasted buns, with your favorite condiments.

Braised Leg of Venison
Serves 10 to 12

For the best results, prepare one day ahead and cool overnight. Before serving, warm the meat and vegetables in the pan juices. We call this a "one-pot wonder!"

Leg of venison (approximately 6 pounds/2¾ kg)
Salt and pepper
½ cup (125 ml) plus 2 tablespoons (30 ml) olive oil
4 bay leaves
2 small onions, chopped
1 pound (450 g) small turnips, peeled and cut into
　　large chunks
1 pound (450 g) carrots, cut into large chunks
1 pound (450 g) parsnips, peeled and cut into large chunks
1 pound (450 g) sweet potatoes, peeled and cut into
　　large chunks
2 small onions, peeled and cut into large chunks
1 bottle (750 ml) red wine
2½ quarts (2.375 l) chicken stock or broth

RICE:
1 pound (450 g) wild rice
2 small onions, chopped
1 cup (250 ml) shelled hickory or pecan nuts
1 cup (250 ml) dried cherries
2½ quarts (2.375 l) chicken stock or broth
Salt and pepper

Preheat the oven to 350°F (180ºC).

Sprinkle the venison liberally with salt and pepper. In a heavy-bottomed braising pan or Dutch oven over medium heat add ½ cup (125 ml) oil and bay leaves, then venison. Braise each side 5 to 10 minutes until browned. Add the vegetables and cook until softened. Add the red wine and chicken stock.

Cover and bake for 2½ to 3 hours, until the meat falls off bone.

To make the wild rice, sauté onion, rice, nuts, and dried cherries in 2 tablespoons (30 ml) oil on medium heat for 10 minutes. Add the chicken stock to cover. Bring to a boil, lower the heat, and simmer (uncovered) until all the liquid is absorbed. Season with salt and pepper to taste.

Serve the meat with the wild rice, braised vegetables, and pan juices.

Elk Sauerbraten
Serves 14 to 16

Serve with boiled potatoes and braised cabbage.

2 tablespoons (30 ml) vegetable oil
6-pound (2¾ kg) elk roast
2 onions, sliced
2 cups (500 ml) water
1 cup (250 ml) vinegar
¼ cup (60 ml) fresh lemon juice
4 tablespoons (60) ketchup
3 bay leaves
6 whole cloves garlic
2 teaspoons (10 ml) salt
½ teaspoon (2 ml) pepper
12 to 14 gingersnaps, crumbled

Heat the oil in a Dutch oven over medium heat. Add the meat and brown on all sides. Add the onions, water, vinegar, lemon juice, ketchup, bay leaves, garlic, salt, and pepper. Bring to a boil and cook for 8 to 10 minutes. Reduce the heat and simmer for 3½ hours. During the last 30 minutes, stir in the gingersnaps.

Remove the meat from the cooking liquid. Discard the bay leaves and garlic. While slicing the meat, bring the gravy to a boil, reduce the heat, and cook until the liquid is reduced to a desirable consistency. Serve the meat with the gravy.

Venison Bulgolgi Pinwheels
Serves 6

This spicy Korean barbecue is one of our favorite ways to tenderize game, and the intense flavors—all ingredients that can be purchased in a well-stocked supermarket—never fail to delight the uninitiated. One tip to slicing the meat super thin is to partially thaw the frozen meat and slice it on the thickest setting of your mandoline or with a sharp chef's knife.

MARINADE:
½ cup (125 ml) soy sauce
½ cup (125 ml) sugar
2 tablespoons (30 ml) sweetened rice wine (optional)
1 tablespoon (15 ml) toasted sesame seeds
1 tablespoon (15 ml) grated peeled fresh ginger
3 cloves garlic, minced
2 small red chiles, seeded and minced
1 teaspoon (5 ml) dark sesame oil
1 bunch scallions, thinly sliced

2 pounds (900 g) venison, hind or shoulder piece, cut into 18 strips (1 x 6 to 8 inches /2.5 x 15 to 20.5 cm) with the grain, ½ inch (1.5 cm) thick

One hour before barbecuing, combine the soy sauce, sugar, rice wine, if using, sesame seeds, ginger, garlic,

chiles, sesame oil, and scallions in a large nonreactive bowl. Add the meat and marinate in the refrigerator.

Prepare a hot fire in a gas or charcoal grill. The temperature should read 450°F (230°C), or the heat should be so intense that it is impossible to hold a hand above the grate for more than a few seconds.

Roll strips of meat into pinwheels and skewer, making three pinwheels per skewer for one serving. Pour the remaining marinade into a small saucepan and simmer over medium heat for 20 minutes.

Meanwhile, grill the pinwheels, 5 minutes per side for rare, or longer as desired. Serve with the cooked marinade on the side.

Venison with Balsamic Vinegar
Serves 4

Serve with wild rice and a cooked vegetable, such as carrots.

1 to 1½ pounds (450 to 675 g) trimmed venison loin
  or rump steak pieces
Salt and pepper
3 tablespoons (45 ml) clarified butter or vegetable oil,
  divided
1 to 1½ cups (250 to 375 ml) thinly sliced red or
  yellow onion
¼ cup (60 ml) balsamic vinegar
½ cup (125 ml) beef stock or broth or water
4 tablespoons (60 ml) cold butter, divided

Lightly season all sides of the meat with salt and pepper.

In a large skillet, heat 2 tablespoons (30 ml) of the clarified butter over high heat. Add the meat to the pan and brown on all sides, 1 to 3 minutes, depending on size of pieces. Cook the meat in separate batches if necessary to avoid crowding in pan. Remove the meat to a cutting board.

Add the remaining 1 tablespoon (15 ml) clarified butter to the pan and sauté the onions until nicely browned, 6 to 8 minutes. Add the vinegar and cook until the pan is dry. Add the stock and bring to a boil, stirring to scrape any glaze from the pan bottom. Season with a pinch of salt and pepper.

Add 2 tablespoons (30 ml) of the cold butter to the pan and whisk in. Remove the sauce from the heat and whisk in the remaining 2 tablespoons (30 ml) butter.

Slice the meat thinly (⅙ inch/4.2 mm) across the grain. Place slices on plates and pour the sauce around.

Lamb Chops with Chinese Black Rice

Serves 4

RICE:
3/4 cup (175 ml) black rice (available from Asian food stores)
1 1/2 cups (375 ml) water
3/4 teaspoon (4 ml) salt, divided
2 tablespoons (30 ml) vegetable oil
1 bunch scallions, chopped (about 3/4 cup/175 ml)
1 tablespoon (15 ml) minced peeled fresh ginger

LAMB CHOPS:
2 tablespoons (30 ml) fresh lime juice
3 cloves garlic, finely chopped
3/4 teaspoon (4 ml) salt
1/2 teaspoon (2 ml) black pepper
1/4 teaspoon (1 ml) ground cumin
1/4 teaspoon (1 ml) ground cardamom
2 tablespoons plus 2 teaspoons (40 ml) olive oil, divided
8 (1/2 to 3/4 inch/1.3 to 2 cm thick) lamb chops, about
   2 pounds (900 g)

Rinse the rice in a sieve under cold water. Bring the rice, water, and 1/2 teaspoon (2 ml) salt to a boil in a 1 1/2- to 2-quart (1.5 to 2 l) saucepan. Turn the heat to low and cook the rice, covered, until tender and most of the water is absorbed, about 30 minutes. Let the rice stand, covered, off the heat for 10 minutes. Over medium heat, sauté scallions in the vegetable oil until soft, about 3 to 4 minutes. Toss scallions and ginger with rice.

Meanwhile, to prepare the lamb, whisk together the lime juice, garlic, salt, pepper, cumin, cardamom, and 2 teaspoons (10 ml) olive oil in a small bowl. Pour into a zippered plastic bag just large enough to hold the lamb. Add the lamb and seal the bag, forcing out excess air. Massage the lamb until it is evenly coated with the marinade. Marinate at room temperature, turning the bag occasionally, for 15 minutes.

Heat 1 tablespoon (15 ml) of the oil in a large nonstick skillet over moderately high heat until hot, but not smoking. Add half the lamb and cook for about 3 minutes on each side for medium rare. Transfer the cooked lamb to a platter. Wipe out the skillet, heat the remaining 1 tablespoon (15 ml) oil and cook the remaining lamb in same manner. Transfer to platter and let stand for 5 minutes.

Serve the chops on a bed of rice.

Clay-Baked Rabbit with Wild Mushroom Sauce

Serves 6

Time to get your old terra-cotta casserole out of deep storage for this satisfying mix of fall gifts. One way to tenderize wild rabbit is to marinate it for a long time. Another way is to cook it using a moist heat method—in this case, in a porous clay pot that has been soaked in water overnight. As it cooks in the oven, the pot tenderizes the contents with steam.

Pairing rabbit with sour cream appears frequently in Central European cuisines. This recipe is an adaptation of the Byelorussian pechenya zayach'i, or rabbit stew. Serve it with potato pancakes, noodles, or dumplings.

4 ounces (120 g) bacon, chopped
2 small rabbits or one large hare, cleaned and cut into pieces
1/2 cup (125 ml) chopped shallots
2 cloves garlic, minced
1 to 2 pounds (450 to 900 g) wild fall mushrooms
   (chanterelles, hen-of-the-woods, chicken-of-the-woods,
   king boletes, etc.), cleaned and sliced
1/4 cup (60 ml) unsalted butter
1 cup (250 ml) pearl onions, peeled
2 parsnips, peeled and diced
1/2 cup (125 ml) chicken stock or broth
1/2 cup (125 ml) dry vermouth
1/4 cup (125 ml) parsley, chopped
2 bay leaves
Sea salt and white pepper
1 cup (250 ml) sour cream

Prepare a clay pot casserole by soaking in water overnight.

In a large sauté pan, fry the bacon over medium-high heat until browned, 2 to 4 minutes. Remove the bacon from the pan with a slotted spoon and reserve. Add the rabbit pieces to the bacon drippings and fry over medium-high heat until browned, 10 minutes on each side, and transfer to the prepared clay pot.

Add unsalted butter to the sauté pan. Add the shallots and garlic to the sauté pan and cook over medium-high heat until softened, 3 minutes. Add the mushrooms and sauté until browned, 10 minutes. Add the pearl onions and parsnips and sauté for 5 minutes more. Finally, add the stock, vermouth, parsley, bay leaves, salt and pepper to taste, and reserved bacon. Bring to a boil. Pour the mixture over the rabbit in the clay pot.

Cover the clay pot and place in a cold oven. Bake at 400°F (200°C) for 45 minutes.

Remove the clay pot from the oven and carefully drain the pan drippings into a bowl. Whisk the sour cream into the drippings and pour back over the rabbit. Return the clay pot, uncovered, to the oven and heat for 5 minutes, then serve.

Venison Medallions with Maple Cinnamon Butter

Serves 6

1½ (375 ml) cups water, divided
¼ cup (60 ml) pure maple syrup
¼ cup (60 ml) apple cider or other vinegar
1 cinnamon stick, crushed
1 cup (250 ml) unsalted butter, softened
½ teaspoon (2 ml) Dijon mustard
1 teaspoon (5 ml) salt, divided
1 teaspoon (5 ml) freshly ground black pepper, divided
½ cup (125 ml) canola oil or other fat, such as bacon grease
1½ to 2 pounds (675 to 900 g) venison loin or leg
   medallions (¼ inch/6 mm thick), silver skin trimmed,
   lightly pounded, or similar amount of chops, trimmed well
1½ teaspoons (7 ml) kosher salt (or coarse sea salt)

In a nonreactive pan, bring 1 cup (250 ml) of the water to a boil with the maple syrup, vinegar, and cinnamon stick. Reduce the heat and simmer until liquid is reduced to about ⅓ cup (75 ml). Strain to remove the cinnamon stick and let cool to room temperature.

Beat the cooled liquid into the softened butter along with the mustard and ½ teaspoon (2.5 ml) each of salt and pepper. Chill the butter. This flavored butter can be made up to several days in advance and kept refrigerated or frozen for several weeks.

Season the meat with the remaining ½ teaspoon (2.5 ml) salt and ½ teaspoon (2.5 ml) pepper.

In a large, heavy-bottomed skillet, heat the oil over high heat until it just begins to smoke. Add the venison and sear for about 1 minute. Turn over and cook for about 45 seconds on the other side. Drain on paper towels briefly, then lay overlapping on a platter or on individual plates. Repeat the process if cooking in batches. Sprinkle with kosher salt.

Remove the pan from heat, drain the oil, and add the remaining ½ cup (125 ml) water to the pan. It should immediately boil from the residual heat in the pan. While it is boiling, scrape up the crusty debris on the bottom of the pan and continue cooking until the liquid is reduced by half. Whisk in the cold maple butter a little at a time to form a smooth, lightly thickened sauce. Spoon the sauce over the meat and serve.

Jamaican "Jerk" Bear or Wild Boar Ribs

Serves 4

BEAR:
2 bear or boar rib racks (12-bone each), split in two
½ cup (125 ml) liquid smoke

JERK SAUCE:
½ onion, chopped
⅔ cup (150 ml) chopped scallions
¼ cup (60 ml) pickled jalapeños
2 cloves garlic
2 tablespoons (30 ml) soy sauce
2 tablespoons (30 ml) dark rum
10 drops Tabasco sauce
1½ teaspoons (7 ml) salt
1½ teaspoons (7 ml) ground allspice
1 teaspoon (5 ml) black pepper
½ teaspoon (2 ml) dried thyme
½ teaspoon (2 ml) ground cinnamon
¼ teaspoon (1 ml) ground nutmeg
1 quart (1 l) tomato-based prepared barbecue sauce

GARNISH:
Pineapple chunks
Sliced scallions

Trim the excess fat from the ribs. Place the ribs in a large roasting pan or large Dutch oven. Add the liquid smoke and cover the ribs with cold water. Cover the pan and bring to a boil over high heat. Lower the heat and simmer until the meat is tender and falling from the bone, about 1½ hours. Check for doneness every 15 minutes. Transfer the ribs to a clean, shallow roasting pan, in a single layer.

To make the jerk sauce, combine the onion, scallions, pickled jalapeños, garlic, soy sauce, rum, Tabasco sauce, salt, allspice, pepper, thyme, cinnamon, and nutmeg in food processor and process until minced. Stir into the barbecue sauce.

Preheat the oven to 450°F (230°C).

Add a small amount of water to bottom of the rib pan (¼ inch/6 mm deep). Pour 1 cup (250 ml) of the jerk sauce over each rack of ribs. Cover the pan with aluminum foil.

Bake the ribs for 15 minutes. Remove the aluminum foil and bake for an additional 5 minutes.

Place the ribs on a large serving platter. Garnish with chunks of fresh pineapple and sliced scallions.

Game Processing

In general, the younger the animal the more tender it will be, whether you harvest it yourself from the wild or purchase it. A crucial factor that affects the quality, freshness, and taste of game is how it is handled in the field, transported, butchered, and stored.

The meat cuts of big game animals parallel closely those of beef and pork. You will find that the meat from wild game animals is always leaner than meat from their domestic counterparts.

For example, if a cut of big game is tender—say from the loin or lower back strap—it should be pan fried quickly on high heat, searing the outside and adding a charred flavor. This technique cooks the meat to medium rare and prevents it from drying. The natural juices remain for flavor.

Less tender cuts from the shoulder, lower rump, and upper back leg can be tenderized by slowly braising or stewing on low heat.

Tip: It is crucial to check the meat often while it cooks.

Venison Meatballs
Makes 30 to 40 meatballs

2 pounds (900 g) ground venison
2 medium eggs
1/2 teaspoon (2 ml) salt
1/4 teaspoon (1 ml) pepper
1 jar (12-ounce/340 g) chili sauce
1 teaspoon (5 ml) fresh lemon juice
1 jar (10-ounce/283 g) grape jelly

Preheat the oven to 350°F (180°C).

Mix the venison, eggs, salt, and pepper in a large bowl. Shape the mixture into small balls.

Combine the chili sauce, lemon juice, and grape jelly in a 9x13-inch (3.5 l) baking pan. Add meatballs and bake, covered, for 1 hour.

Remove the cover and bake for an additional 30 minutes. Transfer to chafing dish and serve hot with toothpicks.

Wild Boar Shoulder with Sage and Onions

Serves 8 to 10

2 medium onions, thinly sliced, divided
15 to 20 fresh sage leaves, thinly sliced, or 3 tablespoons
  (50 ml) dried leaves, divided
6 cloves garlic, crushed
4- to 5-pound (1.8 to 2.25 kg) bone-in wild boar or pork
  shoulder roast, fat trimmed
Sea salt and freshly ground black pepper
1 to 2 cups (250 to 500 ml) chicken stock or broth
2 tablespoons (30 ml) all-purpose flour
2 tablespoons (30 ml) tomato paste

Preheat the oven to 275°F (135°C).

In a large Dutch oven or roasting pan, scatter half the onions, half the sage, and all the garlic along the bottom. Place the meat on the onions and sprinkle with salt and pepper. Top with the remaining onions and sage.

Roast, covered, for 4 to 5 hours, until the meat is very tender and falling from the bone. Carefully remove the meat to a serving platter and keep warm.

Pour the onions and pan juices into a large glass measuring cup; skim the fat from the surface and reserve 2 tablespoons (30 ml). Add enough broth to the juices in the measuring cup to measure 3 cups (750 ml).

Pour the reserved fat back into the Dutch oven. Stir in the flour to make a paste and cook over medium heat for 2 to 3 minutes' reduce until thickened. Stir in the onions, pan juices, and tomato paste; heat to boiling. Boil, uncovered, until mixture is reduced to about 2 cups (500 ml), about 8 to 10 minutes. Season to taste with salt and pepper.

Carve the meat and serve with the gravy.

Bison Burger with Blue Cheese and Cherry Chutney

Serves 4

If you have fresh-picked cherries, you'll want to use them for this recipe. Their tart, succulent flavor melds perfectly with the pungent blue cheese, melting over the coarsely textured, sweet buffalo meat.

CHUTNEY:
1 tablespoon (15 ml) extra virgin olive oil
1 cup (250 ml) pitted Bing cherries
1 cup (250 ml) pitted Rainier cherries
1/4 cup (60 ml) balsamic vinegar
1 1/2 cups (375 ml) red zinfandel or other dry red wine
2 tablespoons (30 ml) dark brown sugar
2 tablespoons (30 ml) minced shallot
1/4 cup (60 ml) chopped fresh thyme
1/4 cup (60 ml) chopped fresh flat-leaf parsley
Zest of 2 lemons, minced
Sea salt and cracked black pepper

BURGERS:
2 pounds (900 g) ground bison meat
1 1/2 ounces (45 g) blue cheese, crumbled

BREAD:
1 tablespoon (15 ml) minced garlic
1/4 cup (60 ml) extra virgin olive oil
4 slices ciabatta bread (1 inch/2.5 cm thick)

For the chutney, heat the olive oil in saucepan over medium heat until smoking. Add the cherries and sauté for 2 to 3 minutes. Add the balsamic vinegar and reduce by half. Then add the red wine, brown sugar and shallots and continue to reduce until the wine/sugar mixture thickens to syrup consistency.

Remove from heat and stir in chopped thyme, flat-leaf parsley and lemon zest. Taste and adjust seasoning with sea salt and pepper. Set aside.

For the burgers, form the bison meat into four 1/2-pound (225 g) patties. Season with salt and pepper. Set aside.

In a small bowl, mix the garlic and olive oil. Brush the Ciabatta bread pieces with the oil mixture. Season with salt and pepper.

Prepare a very hot grill. Toast the bread until brown on both sides, but still soft in the center. Remove from grill.

Place the burgers on the grill and cook 4 to 5 minutes per side for medium doneness. Halfway through grilling, flip the patties and divide blue cheese evenly between the 4 patties; cover and finish grilling to your preferred doneness.

Place one burger on each piece of bread, top with chutney and serve "open-faced" immediately.

Bear Wellington Astoria

Serves 4

BEAR WELLINGTON:
2 tablespoons (30 ml) oil
4 bear tenderloin medallions (6 ounces/170 g each)
Salt and pepper
2 tablespoons (30 ml) butter
8 ounces (225 g) chanterelle mushrooms, finely chopped
1 tablespoon (15 ml) minced shallot
1 tablespoon (15 ml) chopped fresh parsley
4 puff pastry sheets (5 inch/12 cm square each)
1 large egg beaten with 1 tablespoon (15 ml) water (optional)
Fresh chopped chives, to garnish

Astoria Sauce:
1/4 cup (60 ml) butter
8 ounces (225 g) chanterelle mushrooms, roughly chopped
1 tablespoon (15 ml) minced shallot
2 tablespoons (30 ml) burgundy
1 beef bouillon cube
1 tablespoon (15 ml) sour cream
1 1/2 cups (375 ml) heavy cream
Salt and pepper

Preheat the oven to 450°F (230°C). Lightly grease a sheet pan.

To prepare the Wellingtons, heat the oil in a sauté pan over high heat. Season the bear tenderloin medallions with salt and pepper and sear until medium-rare, about 3 minutes per side. Remove the medallions and reserve. Add the butter to the pan. Add the mushrooms and shallot and sauté for about 3 minutes or until tender. Stir in the parsley. Remove from heat and allow to cool.

Spread the mushroom mixture over bear medallions. Place 1 medallion in center of each puff pastry sheet. Fold each corner and side of pastry over medallion using a small amount of water to seal the pastry. The medallion should be completely encased in pastry. Place the Wellingtons seam-side-down on the prepared sheet pan. If desired, brush the egg wash over the top of pastry for a more golden-brown appearance.

Bake the Wellingtons for 12 to 14 minutes, until the pastry is puffed and golden brown.

While the Wellingtons bake, prepare the sauce. Melt the butter in a large sauté pan over medium heat. Add the mushrooms and shallot and sauté 3 to 5 minutes until tender. Add the burgundy and bouillon cube and cook until reduced slightly. Stir in the sour cream and heavy cream. Bring to a boil and reduce until a saucelike consistency is reached. Season with salt and pepper.

To serve, spoon equal amounts of sauce on four plates. Place one pastry-encrusted medallion in the center of each pool of sauce. Garnish with fresh chives.

Game Birds

Whether it's wingshooting for upland game, water fowling for ducks and geese, or matching wits with the cagey wild turkey, bringing birds home is a glorious accomplishment. Even as the hunt is finished, the fanfare continues.

Game birds offer a spectacular range of flavors in high-quality table fare. Wild birds are leaner and denser, with a unique and more satisfying flavor than domesticated varieties.

These birds always warrant cooking that involves revelry and reverence, as they are blessings from the sky.

Pheasant Breast Roulade
Serves 2

ROASTED VEGETABLES:
1 head garlic
2 carrots, diced
1 rutabaga, peeled and diced

PHEASANT:
1 (2 pounds/900 g) pheasant
2 slices bacon, diced

STUFFING:
2 slices bread, dried and diced
2 tablespoons (30 ml) butter, softened
4 dried figs, cut into halves
2 tablespoons (30 ml) golden raisins
1 tablespoon (15 ml) fresh sage, snipped into very small pieces
  (use dried if fresh is not available)

SAUCE:
2 tablespoons (30 ml) red wine vinegar
1 tablespoon (15 ml) butter
1/4 cup (60 ml) honey

Preheat the oven to 350°F (180°C).

Cut the top third off the garlic head to expose the cloves. Wrap in aluminum foil. Roast for about 45 minutes, until soft. Squeeze the garlic out of its casing like toothpaste. Mash it with a fork. Measure out 1 tablespoon (15 ml) for the stuffing and set aside. Reserve remaining garlic for another use.

Meanwhile, wrap the carrots and rutabaga together in aluminum foil. Roast for 25 minutes. Keep warm. Increase the oven temperature to 375°F (190°C).

Meanwhile, on a cutting board, pound and flatten the pheasant breasts* to about 1/2 inch (1.5 cm) in thickness. Keep the two breasts connected and skin attached.

On another surface, spread out the bacon pieces to match the shape of the pounded breasts. Lay the meat down over the bacon and press the entire surface area, helping the bacon stick to the skin of the meat.

Make the stuffing by mixing together the bread, butter, figs, raisins, sage, and reserved roasted garlic. Spread the mixture evenly over the meat. Starting from one end, roll up into a cylinder. Transfer the meat roll into a Dutch oven. Roast for 20 minutes, until the internal temperature reaches at least 160°F (70°C).

When the meat is done, transfer to a cutting board.

To make the sauce, set the Dutch oven with the meat drippings over medium heat. Add the vinegar, butter, and honey. Scrape the little bits of meat off the bottom of the pan with a spatula to mix with liquids. When emulsified, the sauce takes on a blush-brown hue; and the flavor is beautifully complex.

To serve, slice the roulade and arrange on individual serving plates. Drizzle a little sauce around the perimeter of the plate and over each serving of roulade. Serve with the carrots and rutabaga.

Set aside rest of pheasant meat to freeze and use later for soup stock.

Stew of Smoked Chukar Partridge

Serves 4

3 cups (12 ounces/340 g) smoked chukar partridge
  breast, diced

STOCK:
2 ribs celery, coarsely chopped
1 large onion, coarsely chopped
3 to 5 carrots, coarsely chopped
1 cup white wine or water
2 bay leaves (optional)

STEW:
2 acorn squash, halved and seeded
Olive oil
Salt
1/2 cup (125 ml) diced red potato, scrubbed well
1/4 cup (60 ml) diced rutabaga
1/4 cup (60 ml) diced fresh parsnip
1/4 cup (60 ml) diced carrot
1/4 cup (60 ml) diced onion
1/4 cup (60 ml) diced celery

1/4 cup (60 ml) melted butter
3/4 cup (75 ml) all-purpose flour
2 tablespoons (30 ml) tomato paste
2 tablespoons (30 ml) chopped parsley
1 tablespoon (15 ml) kosher salt
1/2 teaspoon (2 ml) cayenne pepper
Blue cheese, crumbled

Marinate the breast meat in the salt brine overnight. Smoke for about 15 minutes. Be careful not to overcook, as the breasts alone have a larger surface area than a whole bird. Set aside 3 cups diced smoked partridge breast meat and reserve any remaining meat for another use.

Preheat oven to 350°F (180°C).

To make the stock, place the chukar carcasses (breast removed) in a shallow roasting pan. Roast for about 30 minutes, stirring occasionally, until well browned. Transfer the carcasses to a large stockpot with the celery, onion, and carrots. Deglaze the hot roasting pan by adding the wine and scraping up any remaining browned bits with a spatula. Add the liquid to the pot along with enough water to cover the solids and bay leaves, if using. Cover and simmer for

about 4 hours to allow the ingredients to break down and flavor the broth. Let cool and refrigerate overnight. The next day, skim the fat that has surfaced on the top with a slotted spoon. Remove all solids from the pot and discard. Strain the broth through cheesecloth to catch any remaining fat, vegetable, and meat bits. Set aside 6 cups (1.5 l) stock and reserve any remainder for another use.

Preheat the oven to 350°F (180°C).

To prepare the stew, brush the squash flesh with olive oil, sprinkle with salt, and place skin-side-up, on a baking sheet. Roast for about 30 minutes, until just soft. Set aside.

Combine the potatoes, rutabagas, parsnips, and carrots in salted water to cover and boil until tender, 5 to 10 minutes. Then sauté the onion and celery in the butter (not previously melted). Stir in the flour to make a roux, then add the broth.

Pour the reserved stock into a large saucepan. In a small bowl, stir the melted butter into the flour until thoroughly blended. Whisk the flour-butter mixture into the cold stock, then start heating the stock, and stir continuously until it begins to thicken. Cook the stock over medium heat for 15 minutes, stirring frequently.

Stir in reserved partridge meat, vegetables, tomato paste, parsley, kosher salt, and cayenne. Cook over medium heat until all are hot throughout, about 8 minutes.

Put one squash half onto each serving plate. Ladle the stew into the squash, top with a few crumbles of blue cheese and serve.

Carolina Doves
Serves 4

Serve with rice or grits, biscuits, and greens.

½ cup (125 ml) plus 2 tablespoons (30 ml) all-purpose flour, divided
Salt and pepper
16 boneless skinless dove breasts
2 tablespoons (30 ml) butter
2 tablespoons (30 ml) canola oil
Water

Put ½ cup (125 ml) flour in a brown paper bag. Season with salt and pepper. Add the doves and shake in the bag to coat well.

Melt the butter in the canola oil in a large skillet over medium-high heat. Add the birds and brown on all sides. Add enough water to come halfway up on the doves. Cover and simmer for 1 to 1½ hours, until the doves are tender. Remove the doves and keep warm.

Stir together the remaining 2 tablespoons (30 ml) flour with 2 tablespoons (30 ml) water to make a smooth paste. Add to the liquid in the pan and cook over medium heat, stirring, until thickened, 5 minutes

To serve, arrange the doves on a serving platter and spoon the gravy over.

Deep-Fried Turkey

If you love wild turkey, you should try deep frying it. You can keep it simple and fry it plain: Dry the bird inside and out to avoid splattering. The outer skin will turn golden brown and a bit crispy.

Or you can use a marinade, injecting it throughout the breasts, thighs, and legs. Pull the needle out as the liquid goes in. This can be done 15 minutes before frying, or 2 hours in advance to let the liquid migrate through the meat.

Your third option is to use a spice rub on the outside of the bird for a savory, crispy skin.

In a nutshell: To fry, immerse the bird in 350°F (175°C) oil. Average cooking time is 3 to 3½ minutes per pound. To test doneness, use a deep-fry thermometer in the thigh. Temperature should reach 180°F (82°C).

Duck Hunting

The cool November sky gradates from slate blue-gray to pale yellow, pink, and fiery orange on the horizon. Sitting in a duck blind at sunrise, admiring this tranquil picture, a water fowler patiently awaits a winged prospect to venture skyward over the marsh.

Duck hunting is an art to be forever mastered: noticing the nuances of wind, listening to subtle sounds, timing, calling, properly rigging for the unique situation at hand, and attempting to understand these dabbling and diving creatures.

Along with this respect for the wild comes a special appreciation for the foods from nature.

Pan-Smoked Duck
Serves 12

To pan-smoke the duck, you will need five pieces of grapevine (4 inches/10 cm long) without leaves or fruitwood twigs, commercial smoking chips, or green tea to provide the smoke.

PAN-SMOKED DUCK:
2 tablespoons (30 ml) coarse salt
2 tablespoons (30 ml) brown sugar
4 skinless and boneless duck breast halves (6 ounces/170 g each)
Sunflower oil, for greasing

SUNCHOKE POTATO DILL WAFERS:
1 large baking potato, well scrubbed, grated
8 medium sunchokes, well scrubbed, grated
1 small onion, grated
2 tablespoons (30 ml) fresh dill leaves, 1 tablespoon (15 ml) dried dill,
    or ½ tablespoon (7 ml) dried yarrow leaves
1 tablespoon (15 ml) coarse salt
Olive oil spray
Egg whites
All-purpose flour

TOPPING:
Chokecherry jam
Scallions, sliced (tender green and white parts)

To prepare the duck, combine the coarse salt and brown sugar and rub into flesh of the duck. Marinate for 1 hour at room temperature. Pat the meat dry with a paper towel and rub with the oil.

To pan-smoke the duck, place wood in the pan and add props to keep a rack about 1 inch (2.5 cm) or so above the pan bottom. Try tuna cans with the ends removed or wads of aluminum foil. Place a greased rack on the props, and arrange the meat to allow smoke to circulate around each piece. Cover with a lid, weighting the lid if necessary for a tight fit. Place the pan over high heat. Lower the heat to medium when the smoking begins. Smoke the duck for 17 minutes. Remove from the heat and cool. The smoked duck will keep for 1 week in refrigerator.

To make the sunchoke-potato wafers, combine the potato, sunchokes, onion, dill, and salt in a medium bowl and mix well. Let stand for 10 minutes.

Preheat the oven to 450°F (230°C).

Place a baking sheet in the oven. Cut two pieces of aluminum foil as large as the baking sheet. Spray oil on foil and set aside.

After 10 minutes, drain the liquid from the grated vegetables by squeezing handfuls over bowl, then place into middle of loosely woven cloth towel or cheesecloth. Gather the corners of cloth to enclose the vegetables, hold it over a sink, and wring, twist, and squeeze the ball of vegetables as tightly as possible, milking out liquid until the vegetables are dry. Open the towel, rearrange the grated mass, and repeat until quite dry.

Place the grated vegetables loosely in a measuring cup.

For every ½ cup (125 ml) of vegetables, add 2 tablespoons (30 ml) egg white and 2 tablespoons (30 ml) flour. Mix well. Drop the mixture by the tablespoon (15 ml) onto the oiled aluminum foil and flatten with fork. Spray generously with olive oil spray. Place the foil on top of the preheated baking sheet.

Bake for 10 minutes, turn over the wafers, and return to bake for 10 minutes more, until completely browned. Remove the wafers to a wire rack to cool. The wafers keep for several hours at room temperature. (If you are making the wafers ahead of time, cool completely, place in airtight container, and store in refrigerator for up to 1 week or in the freezer up to 1 month. Reheat in 350°F/180°C oven to re-crisp.)

To serve, cut the smoked duck breast in half lengthwise and slice diagonally into ¼-inch (6 mm) size slices. Arrange the duck on the wafers. Add a dollop of chokecherry jam and garnish with thin rounds of scallion.

Variation: Trout. Replace the duck with 2 whole dressed trout with skin, fresh or thawed, weighing 1 pound/450 g each and pan smoke for 20 minutes. Prepare the sunchoke-potato wafers as above. Peel the skin from the smoked trout, remove the head and bones, and divide into bite-size pieces. Arrange the trout on wafers and add a dollop of sour cream mixed with fresh dill. Garnish with red radish matchsticks.

Duck with Cranberry and Black Pepper Sauce

Serves 4

4 boneless skinless duck breasts (6-ounce/170 g each)
1 (5 ml) teaspoon kosher salt or coarse sea salt, divided
1 cup (250 ml) cranberries or lingonberries (fresh or frozen)
2 tablespoons (30 ml) brown sugar
2 tablespoons (30 ml) pure maple syrup
1 cup (250 ml) water
½ cup (125 ml) chicken or beef stock or broth
1½ tablespoons (22 ml) whole black peppercorns
3 tablespoons (50 ml) clarified butter or olive oil*
¼ cup (60 ml) butter, cut into four pieces (optional)

Season the duck breasts with ½ teaspoon (2 ml) of the salt and set aside to come to room temperature.

Combine the cranberries, brown sugar, maple syrup, water, stock, and ½ teaspoon (2 ml) salt in a saucepan and bring to a boil. Lower the heat so the mixture boils steadily. Cook for 5 minutes, then begin mashing berries with a fork while the mixture cooks for another 5 minutes or so.

Crush the peppercorns and whisk into the sauce. Cover the pan and let steep for 10 minutes.

Place a strainer over another saucepan and pour the sauce through strainer, pushing to get as much pulp through as possible. Discard the solids (the skins and larger bits of pepper). Gently reheat the sauce and keep warm.

Heat the clarified butter in a large heavy skillet over medium-high heat. Add the duck breasts, skin-side-down. Cook over medium-high heat for 2 to 3 minutes, until browned. Turn over and cook for 2 to 3 minutes, until brown on the second side. The meat should not be cooked past medium-rare (or medium if farm-raised duck is used instead of wild duck).

Remove the breasts from the pan and place skin-side-up on a cutting board. Let rest for 2 minutes.

Whisk the butter into the sauce (or you can leave out if fat is a concern).

Slice each breast diagonally across the grain into 5 or 6 slices and place on platter or individual plates. Spoon the sauce around and serve.

See note about clarified butter on "Grouse with Mushrooms," page 83.

Grouse with Mushrooms

Serves 4

You can use regular white or brown button mushrooms or any combination of mushrooms. Shiitake, oyster, or chanterelle are sometimes available in supermarkets and co-ops. Other foraged mushrooms, such as morels, also can be used.

4 boneless grouse breasts (6-ounce/170 g each)
1½ teaspoon (7 ml) kosher or sea salt, divided
½ teaspoon (2 ml) ground black pepper, divided
3 tablespoons (50 ml) clarified butter or oil, plus more as needed*
8 ounces (225 g) mushrooms, cleaned and trimmed
2 cloves garlic, lightly crushed
1 tablespoon (15 ml) balsamic vinegar
½ cup (125 ml) chicken or beef stock or broth
½ cup (125 ml) heavy whipping cream
Sprig of fresh rosemary (optional)
¼ cup (60 ml) butter, cut into 4 pieces

Season the breasts with ¾ teaspoon (3 ml) salt and ¼ teaspoon (1 ml) pepper and let rest at room temperature for 10 to 15 minutes.

In a large heavy skillet, heat the clarified butter over medium-high heat. Add the seasoned breasts and cook until well browned on one side for 5 to 10 minutes, then turn and cook until well colored on the other side. The meat should still be very juicy. Transfer to a cutting board and cover with a piece of aluminum foil and a towel, to rest while the sauce is prepared.

Return the pan with any remaining clarified butter to medium-high heat. (Add a little more clarified butter if the pan appears dry.) Add the mushrooms and garlic and sauté, stirring occasionally, for 1 to 2 minutes, until lightly browned. Add the vinegar and cook until it is all reduced and absorbed.

Add the broth and reduce by half. The juices from the mushrooms will be rendering out at this point, so reducing the liquid will take a couple of minutes. Add the cream and rosemary sprig, if using, and continue reducing until the sauce is slightly thickened.

Remove the sauce from the heat and whisk in the remaining salt and pepper and the butter.

Remove the garlic cloves and the sprig of rosemary and discard.

Slice each breast diagonally across the grain into four pieces and place on a platter or individual plates. Spoon the sauce and the mushrooms around the meat. Serve immediately.

*Clarifying butter is basically a simple process of separating the water and milk solids from the actual butterfat. To make clarified butter, cube the butter and melt in a saucepan over low heat. There is no need to stir; pay close attention to prevent burning. Move the pan back and forth gently to melt all of the butter. Keep over very low heat for about 15 minutes. Pour through a fine strainer and reserve the clear yellow liquid, which is the clarified butter.

Grouse Hunting

There are very few things in this world that make you feel more connected to your outdoor world than bringing back what you went out for. Sometimes you stumble upon an unexpected treasure along the way. It brings great pleasure as you work with your find in the kitchen, and ultimately enjoy it on the table.

Ironically, the ruffed grouse's own diet includes wild edibles that beautifully accompany many fall upland game bird meals. Grapes, cranberries, pincherries, hazelnuts, and mushrooms can all serve as the beginnings of many tasty side dishes, sauces, and dressings.

Cajun Pheasant Lasagna

Serves 8

1 pound (450 g) boneless pheasant, boned, cut into ½-inch (1.5 cm) cubes
1 pound (450 g) spicy Italian pork sausage
2 tablespoons (30 ml) Cajun seasoning
½ cup (125 ml) finely chopped onion
¼ cup (60 ml) chopped red, yellow, or green bell pepper
2 tablespoons (30 ml) chopped garlic
½ teaspoon (1.5 cm) fresh oregano
2 (10-ounce/280 g) bottles white Alfredo sauce
½ cup (125 ml) freshly grated Parmesan cheese
16 lasagna noodles
2 cups (500 ml) shredded mozzarella cheese

Combine the pheasant, sausage, and Cajun seasoning in large skillet over medium-high heat. Cook until no longer pink, 5 to 7 minutes. Remove from the pan with a slotted spoon and set aside.

In juices remaining in the pan, sauté the onion, bell pepper, garlic, and oregano over medium heat, for 5 minutes until translucent. Stir into the meat mixture. Add the Alfredo sauce and Parmesan cheese, mix well.

In a large pot of salted boiling water, partially cook the lasagna noodles. Drain well.

Preheat the oven to 350°F (180°C). Grease a 9x13-inch (3.5 l) baking dish.

Arrange a layer of noodles in the baking dish. Cover with the sauce and meat mixture. Top with mozzarella. Repeat the layers with the remaining noodles, sauce, and cheese.

Bake for 1 hour, or until thoroughly heated. Let rest 10 minutes before cutting into squares and serving.

Goose with Chokecherry Sauce

Serves 8 to 10

1 goose, 10 to 12 pounds (4.5 to 5.5 kg), skinned
Olive oil
Freshly ground black pepper
Bacon strips

SAUCE:
2 tablespoons (30 ml) butter
2 cloves garlic, minced
½ cup (125 ml) dry red wine
½ cup (125 ml) chokecherry jelly

Preheat the oven to 350°F (180°C).

Rub the goose with olive oil, grind black pepper over the top, and wrap in bacon strips. Place the goose in a shallow roasting pan, breast-side-up.

Roast for 1½ to 2 hours, until the temperature of the breast reaches 180°F (82°C) with an instant-read thermometer, and the juices run clear.

To make the sauce, melt the butter in a small saucepan over medium-high heat. Add the garlic and sauté for 2 to 3 minutes; do not allow to brown. Pour in the wine. Bring the mixture to a gentle simmer and add the jelly. Simmer until the jelly has completely liquefied. Keep warm.

Slice the goose and serve topped with the chokecherry sauce and bits of bacon.

Red-Cooked Duck

Serves 3 to 4

"Red cooking" is a traditional Chinese technique that adapts particularly well to ducks. The meat becomes fall-off-the-bone tender with a sweet-salty taste. Cut up whole ducks for this dish or just use the legs, thighs, and wings, saving the breasts for another dish. Skinned duck is used in this dish, but skin-on (plucked) duck works fine. The broth is flavored with star anise, a dried spice that can be found in the Asian department at large supermarkets or specialty markets. It is the fruit of a small evergreen tree native to China and has a pungent, licoricelike flavor.

2 cups (500 ml) soy sauce
1 cup (250 ml) chicken stock or broth
3 tablespoons (50 ml) dry sherry (optional)
2 cloves garlic
2 thick slices peeled fresh ginger
1 star anise or ¼ teaspoon (1 ml) anise extract
½ cinnamon stick
2 to 3 pounds (1 to 1.5 kg) duck, cut into serving-size pieces
Chopped scallions or crushed peanuts, to garnish

Combine the soy sauce, chicken stock, sherry, garlic, ginger, star anise, and cinnamon in a large nonreactive saucepan; stir to combine. Add the duck. Bring to a gentle boil over medium-high heat. Lower the heat and simmer for 1¾ to 2½ hours, rearranging and turning duck pieces frequently so all sides cook evenly. The duck is done when the meat is very tender and almost falling off the bone; it will be a rich brownish red color (smaller ducks will cook more quickly than large ducks).

Remove the duck pieces from the sauce; set aside and keep warm. Strain and degrease the sauce (a gravy separator does a fine job of degreasing).

When the duck pieces are cool enough to handle, pull the meat from the bones and pull apart into small chunks or large shreds. Serve the duck with some of the sauce. For extra color, sprinkle the duck with chopped scallions or crushed peanuts.

Pheasant Hunting

The majesty of this bird's plumage exudes the dramatic essence of autumn and winter. Wild pheasant is by far one of the finest table fare examples among game birds.

The breast meat is ample, white, and tender. The leg and thigh meats are dark and firm. White and dark meat served together is a lovely, balanced combination of taste and texture.

The elegant "pheasant under glass" has been popular since days gone by. The meat was roasted and put under a glass dome to keep it moist, from kitchen to table. A classic sauce often included white wine with a little brandy or cognac. Thus, the lifting of the glass let escape a memorable olfactory experience, stimulating the taste buds.

Pheasant Wild Mushroom Cacciatore
Serves 6

Translated from the Italian, cacciatore means "hunter-style." It is a savory ragù blending the best of early fall bounty. While any game can be featured in this piquant dish, pheasant is an ideal choice. The mild, dense flesh marries well with the complex flavors of dusky wild mushrooms and rich, mellow tomato and herb sauce. Do not omit the wine; alcohol releases flavors into the sauce that water cannot, especially from tomato.

¼ cup (60 ml) fruity extra virgin olive oil, divided
¼ cup (60 ml) shallots, minced
2 onions, chopped
3 cloves garlic, minced
1 to 2 pounds (450 to 900 g) meaty, wild fall mushrooms, such as honey
   or boletes, cleaned and sliced
1 cup (250 ml) dry white wine, divided
¼ cup (60 ml) white flour
1 tablespoon (15 ml) sea salt
2 pheasants, cleaned and cut into five pieces each
2 cans (28 ounces/794 g each) or boxes of Italian plum tomatoes, crushed
½ cup (125 ml) kalamata olives, pitted and halved
½ cup (125 ml) Italian parsley, chopped
2 bay leaves
2 tablespoons (30 ml) fresh rosemary, chopped
1 tablespoon (15 ml) fresh sage, minced
½ tablespoon (7 ml) fresh thyme
½ teaspoon (2 ml) red pepper flakes
Salt and pepper to taste

In a 5-quart (5 l) sauté pan, heat 2 tablespoons (30 ml) of olive oil over medium-high heat until hot but not smoking. Add shallots, onion, and garlic. Sauté until translucent, then add mushrooms and sauté for approximately 5 minutes until just beginning to brown.

Add ½ cup (125 ml) of white wine (reserving remainder for later) and simmer for another 5 minutes. Remove from heat and place mushroom mixture in a large kettle.

Combine flour and salt in a plastic bag and place pheasant inside, shaking to coat pieces. Add remaining 2 tablespoons (30 ml) of olive oil to sauté pan and sauté pheasant pieces for a couple of minutes until browned on both sides.

Remove from heat and place in kettle containing mushroom mixture. Add remaining ½ cup (125 ml) of wine, tomatoes, olives, and seasonings to kettle and stir until contents are combined.

Heat on medium-high heat until boiling; reduce heat to low and simmer for 1 hour until pheasant is tender.

Serve hot in bowls.

Brandied Goose

Serves 4 to 6

2 tablespoons (30 ml) butter
2 tablespoons (30 ml) vegetable oil
1 goose (10 to 12 pounds/4.5 to 5.5 kg), cut into
   serving pieces
All-purpose flour
2 cups (500 ml) chicken stock or broth
1 cup (250 ml) beef stock or broth
2 tablespoons (30 ml) prepared steak sauce
¼ cup (60 ml) dry sherry
⅛ teaspoon (.05 ml) dried marjoram
½ teaspoon (2 ml) salt
¼ teaspoon (1 ml) pepper
2 bay leaves
2 tablespoons (30 ml) cornstarch
1 pound (450 g) sweet, pitted cherries with syrup
2 tablespoons (25 ml) brandy

Preheat the oven to 325°F (165°C).

Melt the butter in the oil in a large Dutch oven over medium heat. Coat the goose pieces in flour, add to the Dutch oven, and brown 3 to 5 minutes on each side. Set the goose aside. Add chicken and beef broth, steak sauce, sherry, marjoram, salt, pepper, and bay leaves to the Dutch oven and bring to a boil. Return the goose to the Dutch oven, cover, and roast for 2½ to 3 hours, until tender. Remove the meat from the pan.

To make the sauce, mix cornstarch with cherries and brandy. Slowly add the mixture to the pan juices; stir and place over low heat until sauce is slightly thickened and translucent. Return the goose to the sauce and simmer for 15 minutes.

Serve the goose on a platter with sauce spooned over.

Apple Quail

Serves 3 or 4

Serve the quail on a bed of rice with sautéed apples on the side.

¼ cup (30 g/60 ml) all-purpose flour
½ teaspoon (2 ml) salt, or to taste
⅛ teaspoon (0.5 ml) paprika
6 quail, breasts and legs only
2 to 3 tablespoons 30 to 45 ml) butter
¼ cup (60 ml) chopped sweet onion
1 tablespoon (15 ml) chopped fresh parsley
¼ teaspoon (1 ml) dried thyme or ½ teaspoon (2 ml)
   fresh thyme
1 cup (250 ml) apple juice

Combine the flour, salt, and paprika in a brown paper bag. Add the quail and shake in the bag to coat well.

Melt 2 tablespoons (30 ml) butter in large heavy skillet over medium heat. Add the quail and brown all sides. Push the quail to one side of pan. Add a tablespoon (15 ml) butter if pan is dry. Add the onion and sauté until tender, 5 minutes. Stir in the parsley, thyme, and apple juice. Spoon the pan juices over the quail while bringing to a boil. Lower the heat, cover, and simmer until quail is tender, about 1 hour.

Serve hot with the pan juices spooned over the quail.

Dove Bog

Serves 4 to 6

When preparing the doves, use a game scissors to cut away the legs and shoulders so the entire breast can be pulled free. (Reserve for another use.) Be sure to check the meat thoroughly for bones.

STOCK:
Boneless skinless breasts of 6 dozen doves
1 bay leaf
1 teaspoon (5 ml) garlic salt
Pinch of crushed red pepper flakes
Water

BOG:
1 teaspoon (5 ml) olive oil
½ cup (125 ml) chopped onion
1 cup (250 ml) chopped venison kielbasa or regular kielbasa
1 garlic clove, minced
1 cup (250 ml) long-grain white rice
½ teaspoon (2 ml) kosher salt
½ teaspoon (2 ml) freshly ground black pepper

To prepare the stock, place the breast meat in a Dutch oven. Add the bay leaf, garlic salt, and crushed red pepper flakes. Cover with cold water. Slowly bring to a simmer, cover, and simmer for 2 hours, until meat is tender and falling from the bones.

Strain the stock. Set aside 2½ cups (625 ml) dove stock and 2 cups (500 ml) dove meat. Reserve any extra for another use.

To make the bog, heat the olive oil in a large Dutch oven on medium heat. Add the onion and sauté for 5 minutes until translucent. Add the chopped kielbasa, garlic, and rice and continue sautéing for 1 minute

Add 2 cups (500 ml) of the dove stock, bring to a boil, lower the heat, and cook for 15 minutes. Add the dove meat, salt, pepper and additional ½ cup (125 ml) stock if needed to fully cook.

Cook for 5 more minutes or until the rice is tender.

Serve immediately.

Sweet and Smoky Grilled Duck

Serves 2 to 4

4 cups (1 l) apple juice
4 cups (1 l) cold water
½ cup (125 ml) coarse kosher salt
½ teaspoon (2 ml) Tabasco or other hot sauce
1 or 2 whole ducks, skin on, halved and washed
⅓ cup (75 ml) orange juice
3 tablespoons (50 ml) honey
1 tablespoon (15 ml) chopped fresh rosemary leaves,
   or 1 teaspoon (5 ml) dried
2 teaspoons (10 ml) paprika
½ teaspoon (2 ml) cracked black pepper

Combine the apple juice, water, salt, and Tabasco in large ceramic bowl or stainless-steel pot. Stir until the salt dissolves. Add the duck halves and weigh down with ceramic plate. Cover and refrigerate for 2 hours.

Prepare a hot fire in a charcoal grill by arranging the charcoal in two banks at the sides of the grill. Place a metal pan between the banks of coals and fill the pan with water. Soak a few handfuls of fruitwood chips in water.

When the coals are hot and covered with white ash, remove the duck from the brine and pat dry. Discard the brine. Drain the wood chips and toss half onto coals.

With the grill grate over coals, arrange the duck halves, skin-side-up, over the water pan (not the coals). Cover the grill and cook for 20 to 30 minutes, depending on the size of the ducks. Add the remainder of the wood chips to coals and move the ducks around, keeping them skin-side-up. Cover and cook for another 15 to 30 minutes, depending on the size of the ducks.

Meanwhile, mix the orange juice, honey, rosemary, paprika, and pepper in a small bowl.

After the ducks have cooked for 35 to 60 minutes, turn the ducks skin-side-down and brush with the orange juice mixture. Cover and cook, turning and basting every 5 minutes, for 20 minutes longer.

Serve immediately.

Quail with Currant Sauce

Serves 2 to 3

¼ cup (60 ml) butter
4 quail, cut into serving pieces
½ cup (125 ml) currant jelly
Salt
1 tablespoon (15 ml) brandy, or to taste

Melt the butter in large heavy skillet over low to medium heat. Add the quail and brown slowly 6 to 7 minutes per side. Remove the quail and keep warm.

Add the currant jelly to the skillet and stir well while jelly melts. Season with salt to taste.

Return the birds to the pan and baste with the sauce. Cover and simmer until the quail are tender, about 1 hour. Stir the brandy into the sauce and cook until just heated. Taste to see if more brandy is needed.

Serve immediately with sauce spooned over the quail.

Pheasant Roll-Ups

Serves 6

2 pheasants, boned*
8 ounces (230 g) "sandwich" pepperoni (slices measure
   2½ to 3 inches/6.5 to 7.5 cm) in diameter; pizza
   pepperoni is too small)
1 cup (250 ml) zesty Italian salad dressing

Cut the meat into pieces that are approximately 3 inches (7.5 cm) long and 1½ inches (3.5 cm) wide and the thickness of the breast or leg parts. Rinse the pheasant pieces and pat dry with paper towels.

Wrap each chunk of meat with a slice of pepperoni and secure with a toothpick. Put in a shallow plastic container with lid that seals tight. Pour the salad dressing over the meat. Marinate for 24 hours in the refrigerator, turning the container once or twice to ensure complete coverage with the marinade.

Prepare a charcoal fire on one side of the grill or preheat a gas grill with the burners on high on one side. Place the pheasant pieces over the side without the heat and grill indirectly only long enough so the pheasant chunks are cooked through with no pink center, 5 to 10 minutes.

Serve immediately.

*Can substitute ruffed or blue grouse, whole dove breasts, or quail.

Fish and Seafood

Wild-caught fish are like glistening jewels lifted from a treasure chest. They carry the tastes of their species, as they swim freely, eating the natural flora and fauna of the habitat. Local and international waters brim with a bounty of seafood. As long as their worlds are healthy ones, we reap the benefits—safe, nutritous ingredients and sumptuous table fare.

As the seasons unfold, many menu opportunities arise—from frying fresh perch caught on the ice, to making a shore lunch over an open fire amidst palm trees, to smoking-up the kitchen to blacken some salmon.

Dungeness Crab Salad

Serves 4

This recipe is easy to make and elegant enough to serve for a special occasion but because the crab and avocado forms such a dreamy double date with the asparagus and crunchy sesame seeds, you may want to make it whenever you can get asparagus. Spend the extra money for the best quality crab because it makes a big difference.

VINAIGRETTE:
¼ cup (60 ml) mirin (Japanese rice wine)
¼ cup (60 ml) rice wine vinegar
2 tablespoons (30 ml) brown sugar
1 teaspoon (5 ml) soy sauce
1 teaspoon (5 ml) dark sesame oil

SALAD:
2 ripe avocados, divided
1 pound (450 g) Dungeness crabmeat, picked over
½ cup (125 ml) mayonnaise
1 teaspoon (5 ml) fresh lemon juice
¼ cup (60 ml) finely diced celery, blanched, and shocked
¼ cup (60 ml) finely diced onion, blanched, and shocked
¼ cup (60 ml) finely diced carrot, blanched, and shocked
¼ cup (60 ml) thinly sliced fresh chives
¼ cup (60 ml) thinly sliced scallions (white and tender green parts)
3 tablespoons (50 ml) toasted sesame seeds, divided
½ cup (125 ml) mesclun or other baby salad greens
Lemon wedges
Salt and pepper
1 bunch asparagus, blanched and shocked, cut into 4-inch-long (10 cm) pieces
4 crab claws (optional)

To make the vinaigrette, combine the mirin, rice vinegar, and brown sugar in a small saucepan and cook over medium heat and until it forms a thin syrup that will coat the back of a spoon. Stir in the soy and sesame oil. Set aside.

To make the salad, cut the avocadoes into cubes, setting aside four slices. Toss the reserved slices with a little lemon juice.

In a large mixing bowl, combine the crabmeat with the mayonnaise, lemon juice, avocado chunks, celery, onion, carrot, chives, and scallions. Set aside 1 teaspoon (5 ml) sesame seeds and add the remainder. Gently combine. Set aside.

Dress the greens with a little of the vinaigrette and squeeze on a bit of the lemon. Season with a little salt and pepper.

In a separate mixing bowl, toss the asparagus with 1 tablespoon (15 ml) of the vinaigrette and the reserved 1 teaspoon (5 ml) sesame seeds.

To serve, arrange the asparagus in the center of four chilled plates. Add a scoop of the crab mixture on the asparagus so the tips are visible. Top the crab with an avocado slice and then a small tangle of the greens. Drizzle some of the vinaigrette on either side of the salad, garnish with the crab claws, and serve immediately.

Breaded Perch Fillets
Serves 4

BREADING:
1 cup (250 ml) panko (Japanese-style fresh bread crumbs)
1 cup (250 ml) unseasoned dried bread crumbs
¼ cup (60 ml) toasted sesame seeds
2 tablespoons (30 ml) cracked black pepper
1 tablespoon (15 ml) garlic powder
1 tablespoon (15 ml) onion powder
1 tablespoon (15 ml) paprika
¾ cup (200 ml) half-and-half

FISH:
3 tablespoons (50 ml) peanut oil
1 pound (450 g) perch fillets
2 tablespoons (30 ml) unsalted butter
4 cloves garlic, roasted*
1 large shallot or 1 small onion

Combine the panko, bread crumbs, sesame seeds, pepper, garlic powder, onion powder, and paprika in a shallow bowl in preparation to dredge fillets before frying. Pour the half-and-half into a second shallow bowl.

Heat the peanut oil in a large skillet over medium heat. While the oil is heating, one by one, dip the fillets in the half-and-half, then dredge in breading mixture and set aside on a platter.

Add the butter, roasted garlic cloves, and shallot to the oil in the skillet. Use a spatula to distribute evenly and cook until slightly brown. Add fish fillets in a single layer. Gently shake the pan back and forth and side to side to prevent scorching. Do not flip fish over repeatedly; nor is it necessary to use tongs to move them around, as they will undoubtedly flake up and fall apart given their delicate texture. Fry on one side for about 7 minutes, flip and fry on the other side for about 2 minutes. Drain oil. Serve immediately.

*Cut the top third off the garlic to expose the cloves. Wrap in aluminum foil. Roast for about 1 hour, until soft and tender.

Best Salmon Ever
Serves 4

If you are cooking outdoors, you can cook the salmon in the same way, but leave the foil open.

1 large or 2 small (2 pounds/900 g) salmon fillets
Salt and pepper
2 large tomatoes, diced
3 large yellow or sweet onions, diced
1 red, yellow, or green bell pepper, diced
1 (4-ounce/113 g) can mild green or jalapeño chiles, drained and minced
½ cup (125 ml) butter
½ cup (125 ml) prepared barbecue sauce

Preheat the oven to 350°F (180°C). Cut a piece of aluminum foil large enough to completely enclose the salmon. Brush with olive oil or coat with nonstick spray.

Sprinkle both sides of the fillet with salt and pepper. Place the salmon on the foil brushed with olive oil. Smother the fillet with the tomatoes, onions, bell pepper, and chiles. Cut the butter into pats and place on the top of the fillet. Pour the barbecue sauce over the top. Close the foil and seal. Place on a baking sheet.

Bake for 25 minutes or until the salmon flakes apart. Serve immediately.

Blackened Salmon
Serves 6

1 tablespoon (15 ml) paprika
2½ teaspoons (12 ml) salt
1 teaspoon (5 ml) cayenne pepper
1 teaspoon (5 ml) garlic powder
1 teaspoon (5 ml) onion powder
¾ teaspoon (4 ml) black pepper
¾ teaspoon (4 ml) white pepper
½ teaspoon (2 ml) dried oregano
½ teaspoon (2 ml) dried thyme
2¼ pounds (1 kg) salmon fillets (6 ounces/170 g each) skin removed
4 tablespoons (60 ml) butter, melted, divided
1 to 2 lemons

Mix together the paprika, salt, cayenne, garlic powder, onion powder, black pepper, white pepper, oregano, and thyme in a shallow bowl. Dredge the fish in the mixture to coat both sides.

Preheat the oven to 400°F (200°C).

Heat a large cast-iron skillet over high heat until smoking hot. Add the fish in a single layer. Pour 1 teaspoon (15 ml) melted butter on top of the fish, being careful of flare-ups. Turn the fish over once a black crust is established, 2 to 4 minutes. Repeat the process to blacken the second side. Once blackened on both sides, transfer the fish to a baking sheet. Squeeze fresh lemon over. Wipe out pan between batches.

Bake for about 20 minutes until desired doneness.

Serve immediatley.

Salmon

Three species of salmon live in the North American Pacific—king, coho, and sockeye.

Born in streambeds—with stamina in their blood—they gradually make their way from river mouth to ocean, often heading far offshore, even to the Gulf of Alaska and the Bering Sea. Eventually they return by "smelling" their way back, swimming against the current and leaping waterfalls to reach their birth streambed. After mating and laying eggs, the salmon's life comes to an end, creating another generation to contribute to the food chain.

The season of the salmon invites us to celebrate their spring run! Some say the best way to cook salmon is on a cedar plank, a tradition in Alaska. Others prefer to poach, grill, bake steam, cure, kipper, or smoke them.

No matter what preparation method you choose, you will find wild salmon to be superior in taste and freshness.

Salmon Tower with Morels

Serves 4

Few things cry spring more than morel mushrooms. Their heady, earthy aroma mixed with the sweetness of the sherry complements the fish quite well. But if you do not have morels, any other mushroom will do just fine.

Also, this is an easy recipe to make, but the rolling of the fish and potatoes adds a lot of time. Those wishing to do so, can cut the preparation time drastically by purchasing tater tots from the store and not rolling the fish....It does make for a glorious presentation though.

½ cup (130 ml) water

1- to 2-pound (450 to 900 g) king salmon fillet, belly intact, skinned, pin bone and all blood lines removed

4 large russet potatoes, peeled, shredded, and chopped

1 teaspoon (5 ml) vitamin C powder*

Canola oil

Unsalted butter

16 to 20 medium morel mushrooms, washed and dried

Salt and pepper

1 shallot, finely diced

¼ cup (60 ml) Spanish oloroso or cream sherry

½ cup (125 ml) stock or broth

1 bunch asparagus, blanched and shocked, cut into 1-inch

1 bunch spinach, trimmed

6 tablespoons (90 ml) chicken stock or broth and/or veal demi-glace

2 teaspoons (10 ml) chopped chives

2 teaspoons (10 ml) chopped fresh parsley

2 teaspoons (10 ml) thinly sliced scallions

Roll up the salmon like a cigar and wrap it tightly in plastic wrap, taking care that there are no air bubbles. Refrigerate for a minimum of 4 hours, or overnight.

Soak the potatoes for 10 minutes in lightly salted water to cover to which you have added the vitamin powder. Drain the potatoes, then wring any moisture from the potatoes and spread a small amount onto a sheet of plastic wrap. Roll the potatoes into long tubes, making them approximately 8 inches (20.5 cm) long with a diameter of about ¾ inch (2 cm). Take care to make the potato tubes snug but not too tight (they will have a gluey texture if they are too tight). Twist the ends to seal and repeat this process until you have used all of the potatoes. Transfer the tubes to a freezer overnight or until fully frozen.

Remove the salmon from the refrigerator and slice off the ends to make them flat (discard). Slice the remaining salmon into 2½-inch-thick (6.5 cm) chunks. Reserve until you are ready to cook.

Preheat the oven to 350°F (180°C).

Begin heating the canola oil in a heavy saucepan to 350°F (180°C). Add the salmon log chunks and rotate them so they brown on all sides. Transfer to the oven and bake for 4 to 5 minutes for medium-rare.

Heat another large skillet over medium heat. Add 1 tablespoon (15 g) of the butter with the mushrooms and season well with salt and pepper. Sauté until the mushrooms are browned, 4 minutes. Add the shallot and sherry. Cook, stirring, and scrape up all the browned bits from the bottom of the pan. Cook until the liquid is nearly gone. Add the stock and 1 tablespoon (15 g) of unsalted butter. Cook until the sauce thickens, about 2 minutes. Add the asparagus and spinach and toss to coat. Keep warm.

Remove the potato tubes from the freezer. Fry these "tots" in batches in the hot oil until golden brown, drain and season with salt.

To serve, arrange the salmon chunks (standing them upright to be a tower) next to the vegetables and sauce and slice the tots in half at a sharp angle lengthwise and crisscross them on the plate. Garnish with chives, parsley, and scallions.

Serve immediately.

* Vitamin C powder is available at most supermarkets and health food stores, where it may be labeled "ascorbic acid." It keeps the potatoes from oxidizing (discoloring).

Pan-Fried Walleye with Morel-Leek Sauce
Serves 2

SEASONED FLOUR:
⅓ cup (75 ml) all-purpose flour
2 tablespoons (30 ml) cornmeal
½ teaspoon (2 ml) onion powder
½ teaspoon (2 ml) paprika
½ teaspoon (2 ml) salt
¼ teaspoon (1 ml) garlic powder (optional)

4 to 6 ramps (wild leeks), trimmed
2 to 3 tablespoons (30 to 50 ml) butter, divided
1½ cups (375 g) coarsely chopped morels
1 cup (250 ml) half-and-half or evaporated skim milk
Fillets from 1 eating-sized walleye, skin removed
Salt and pepper

To make the seasoned flour, combine the flour, cornmeal, onion powder, paprika, salt, and garlic powder, if using, in a zippered plastic bag; shake well and set aside.

Slice the ramp bulbs into ⅛-inch-thick (3 mm) slices; slice the greens into ½-inch-wide (1.3 cm) strips.

To make the sauce, melt about 2 teaspoons (10 ml) of the butter in a small saucepan over medium heat. Add the ramps and sauté for a few minutes until soft. Add the morels and continue cooking until they are just tender, 3 minutes.

Push the mushrooms to the side of the pan, and sprinkle 2 teaspoons (10 ml) of the flour mixture into the juices, stirring constantly to prevent lumps. Cook for about 1 minute, stirring frequently. Stir in the half-and-half. Adjust the heat so the mixture bubbles very gently; simmer while you prepare the fish. Be sure to stir the sauce occasionally while you are cooking the fish.

Dredge the damp fish fillets in the flour. Melt 1 tablespoon (15 ml) of the remaining butter in a large heavy-bottomed skillet over medium-high heat. Shake the excess flour from the fillets and add the fillets to the skillet in a single layer. Reduce the heat slightly and cook until the fish is a rich golden brown on the bottom. If the skillet seems dry, add a bit more butter, then turn fillets and cook until fish is just done, 4 minutes on each side. Sprinkle with salt and pepper to taste.

To serve, transfer the fish to a serving plate. Spoon the sauce over fish and serve immediately.

Panko-Coated Walleye with Pickled Cattail Shoots

Serves 4

SPICY MAYO:
1 cup (250 ml) mayonnaise
2 tablespoons (30 ml) chili paste
2 teaspoons (10 ml) smoked Spanish paprika (pimetón)
Juice and zest of 1 lemon

½ cup (125 ml) rice vinegar
2 tablespoons (30 ml) sugar
2 tablespoons (30 ml) salt
1 teaspoon (5 ml) ground cumin
8 ounces (225 g) fresh tender cattail shoots
Oil, for frying
4 walleye fillets (8-ounce/225 g each)
1 cup (250 ml) buttermilk
1 cup (250 ml) panko (soft Japanese bread crumbs)
Salt and pepper
Paprika, for garnish
Chopped fresh chives, for garnish

To make the spicy mayo, stir together the mayonnaise, chili paste, paprika, and lemon juice and zest. Set aside. Heat the vinegar, sugar salt, and cumin in a large saucepan until the sugar is dissolved. Add the cattail shoots, cook until tender, 5 to 10 minutes. Remove from heat and let cool fully.

Heat oil in a large skillet over medium heat. Dip the fish in the buttermilk, then dredge in the panko. Add to the skillet in a single layer and fry for 3 to 4 minutes per side, until golden brown on each side. Remove the fish, drain on paper towels and keep warm. Drain the oil from the pan. Drain cattail shoots and discard the liquid. Add shoots to pan and sauté quickly, about 30 seconds.

To serve, arrange the fish on plates, top with the cattail shoots and dollop on spicy mayo. Garnish with paprika and fresh chives.

Key West Conch Chowder

Serves 4

4 large conches, ground
4 medium potatoes, peeled and diced
8 cups (2 l) water
¼ pound (120 g) salt pork, left whole
1 large yellow onion, diced
1 green bell pepper, diced
1 clove garlic, minced
1 can (14½-ounce/411 g) diced and drained tomatoes
Salt and pepper

Combine the conch, potatoes, and water in a large saucepan and bring to a simmer.

Meanwhile, in a large skillet, render the fat from the salt pork by frying on low to medium heat about 5 to 10 minutes per side. Discard meat chunk left in pan. Add the onion, pepper and garlic and sauté over medium heat until onion is translucent. Add to the conch and potatoes. Add the tomatoes, season with salt and pepper. Continue to simmer about 10 minutes until the potatoes fall apart.

Walleye

The walleye fishing opener is a long-traditional harbinger of spring. As this nocturnal-feeding fish, with light-sensitive eyes, migrates up the river, it seems the entire earth is pregnant with life.

Walleye is highly sought after in the Great Lakes region, and this member of the perch family is found from Connecticut to North Carolina, westward to Washington State, and north to Hudson Bay.

Light and flaky, moist but not fatty, walleye has a somewhat neutral taste that lends itself well to many recipes.

Halibut

Besides the seasonal movement
from deeper waters in the winter
to shallower waters in the summer,
halibut are known to migrate a
surprising distance. Specimens
tagged in the Bering Sea have been
caught as far south as the coast of
Oregon, a migration of more than
2,000 miles (3,219 km).

Pacific Alaskan halibut are often
considered the best-eating halibut.
The season generally lasts from
March 15 to October 15. This fish's
distinctly delicate, yet rich, flavor
and firm texture with a large grain
lends itself to a gamut of sauces—
fruit mango salsa to beurre blanc to
puttanesca.

Most often eaten as fillets and steaks,
halibut can be prepared in a variety
of ways, including grilling, gently
sautéing, broiling, roasting, and
cooking in liquid.

Tip: As these fish are naturally low
in fat, you will always want to use
some butter, oil, or animal fat when
preparing a meal.

Grilled Sturgeon with Yogurt Marinade
Serves 6

This recipe also works great if you substuitute halibut.

2 cups (500 ml) plain yogurt, divided
1 teaspoon (5 ml) fennel seeds, finely ground
1 clove garlic, minced
1 teaspoon (5 ml) minced peeled fresh ginger
½ teaspoon (2 ml) ground cumin
½ teaspoon (2 ml) ground coriander
¼ teaspoon (1 ml) black pepper
1 teaspoon (5 ml) salt, divided
6 (6-ounce/170 g) skinless sturgeon fillets or halibut fillets with skin,
**   cut 1 inch (2.5 cm) thick**
3 tablespoons (50 ml) finely chopped fresh mint
½ teaspoon (2 ml) finely grated lemon zest
2 heads (bunches) collard greens, ribs removed and blanched

Whisk together 1 cup (250 ml) yogurt with the fennel, garlic, ginger, cumin, coriander, pepper, and ½ teaspoon (2 ml) salt in a shallow baking dish. Coat the fish with the yogurt mixture and marinate, covered, in the refrigerator for 1 hour.

While the fish is marinating, make the sauce. Whisk together the remaining 1 cup (250 ml) yogurt, mint, lemon zest, and remaining ½ teaspoon (2 ml) salt. Set aside. Prepare a medium-hot fire in a charcoal or gas grill.

Lift the fish out of the marinade, letting the excess drip off. Discard the marinade. Grill the fish on a lightly oiled grill rack, turning over once until just cooked through, about 12 minutes total. (If you are using halibut, grill skin-side-down first and grill, turning once, for 8 to 9 minutes total.)

Rest the fish off the grill, on a plate for about 5 minutes. Set fish at the long end of colllard green and roll over. Return to the grill for 1 minute each side. Serve hot, passing the yogurt mint sauce at the table.

Baked Parmesan Halibut
Serves 4 to 6

4 tablespoons (60 ml) butter
1 large onion, cut into thin rings
2 pounds (900 g) halibut fillets
¾ cup (175 ml) Miracle Whip or mayonnaise
⅓ cup (75 ml) freshly grated Parmesan cheese
Seasoned bread crumbs

Melt the butter in a large skillet over medium-high heat. Add the onion and sauté for 4 to 5 minutes until tender.

Preheat the oven to 350°F (180°C).

Line the bottom of a 9x13-inch (3.5 l) baking pan with the onion and butter mixture. Layer with the halibut. Spread the Miracle Whip or mayonnaise over the fillets. Sprinkle with the Parmesan cheese and top with the bread crumbs.

Bake for 30 to 45 minutes, depending on size and thickness of fillets, until opaque and flaky. Serve immediately.

Halibut Enchiladas

Serves 8

SAUCE:
3 cups (750 ml) tomato juice
1 package (1.62-ounce/46 g) powdered enchilada sauce mix

FILLING:
1 tablespoon (15 ml) oil or butter
1 white onion, diced
1½ cups (375 ml) diced red, green, or yellow bell pepper
1 pound (450 g) halibut, cut into ½-inch (1.3 cm) cubes
¼ cup (60 ml) chopped mild green chiles
¼ cup (60 ml) chopped ripe olives
¼ cup (60 ml) grated cheddar cheese
3 to 4 tablespoons (45 to 60 ml) chopped green onions
1 cup (250 ml) prepared salsa, divided

WRAPS:
8 soft corn tortillas (10-inch/25 cm diameter)

To make the sauce, mix the tomato juice with the seasoning mix and set aside.

To make the filling, heat the oil in a large skillet over medium heat. Add the onion, bell pepper, and halibut and sauté about 4 minutes until not quite done; set aside.

Combine the chiles, olives, ¼ cup (60 m) prepared salsa.

Preheat the oven to 350° F (180ºC).

To assemble the enchiladas, brush sauce mixture on one side of the tortillas. Place ½ to ¾ cup (125 to 175 ml) halibut filling in the center of each tortilla, roll up, and place seam-side-down in an 11x7-inch (2 l) baking dish. Top with the remaining sauce and grated cheddar cheese, garnish with green onions and salsa.

Bake for 20 to 30 minutes until the cheese is melted and the enchiladas are heated through. Serve hot.

Day Boat Grouper with Sunny Citrus Hollandaise

Serves 4

SAUCE:
2 cups (500 ml) water, divided
4 egg yolks
8 ounces (230 g/250 ml) unsalted butter, clarified*
½ teaspoon (2 ml) salt
Zest of 1 large orange
1 tablespoon (15 ml) fresh lemon juice
1 tablespoon (15 ml) fresh key lime or regular lime juice

FISH:
2 shallots, diced
2 large cloves garlic, minced
2 tablespoons (30 ml) peanut oil
4 grouper fillets, 6 ounces (170 g) each
Honey

To make the sauce, fill the bottom of a double boiler with about 2 inches (5 cm) of water and heat over low heat to simmer very lightly. Use a whisk to beat the egg yolks and 2 tablespoons (30 ml) water in the top of the double boiler until light and airy. Place over the simmering water and cook to warm the egg mixture, yet maintain its liquid form. Stir for about 3 to 5 minutes until thickened.

Remove from the heat and stir in the clarified butter, a little at a time. Add the salt, orange zest, lemon juice, and lime juice while continuing to stir. If the sauce becomes too thick, stir in 1 to 2 tablespoons (15 to 30 ml) of warm water. Keep warm.

In a stovetop or oven pan (or use sauté pan, then transfer fish to small roaster pan for oven, keeping the lid off), sauté shallots and garlic in peanut oil over medium heat until lightly browned, 3 minutes. Remove most of the garlic and onion bits with a slotted spoon, leaving the flavored oil in the pan.

Add the grouper fillets to pan in a single layer. Increase the heat to high and sear the fish on each side for at least 2 to 3 minutes; adjust the time according to thickness of the fish. Brush the top side of grouper with honey.

Transfer the pan to the broiler and broil for 5 minutes until the top becomes a deep, golden brown. The honey caramelizes in the high heat, giving the fish a sweetness and slightly crisp texture. The meat will turn an opaque white when done. Test with a fork if necessary. Drain the fish.

To serve, drizzle the sauce over fish.

See note about clarified butter in "Grouse with Mushrooms," page 83.

Grouper

Many an angler would agree: If you want to land a big grouper, you must act fast and muscle-up to the moment.

Groupers, especially big ones, are savvy, cunning, and very strong—thus, tough to boat. The slightest nudge of a hook will send them seeking refuge in the structure below, inevitably cutting your line!

One Key West resident, known as Lobster Lee, recently took us on a one-day fishing and dive excursion. We anchored on a reef during the rising tide of late afternoon. After a long fight, Bill landed a big grouper. Lobster Lee, a chef at heart, became excited and inspired.

After filleting the fish, he rummaged through our potpourri of provisions, found some pots and pans and began cooking right there on the boat.

What a treat it was to have grouper fresh from the sea.

Stonecrab

Once you start looking for any kind of crab at the seashore and in the bays, you will be amazed at the many shapes and colors of their bodies and the unique places in which they live.

After hatching, stonecrab larvae spend about 36 days floating with the plankton. They then move into shallow waters near jetties and in coastal bays as they mature.

Stonecrabs have small bodies and only the meat within a claw is eaten. To be harvested, claws must be $2^{1}/_{2}$ inches (6.3 cm) long, measured from the tips of the immovable finger to the first joint. Only one legal-size claw may be removed from a crab and then the crab must be returned immediately to the water, where it often regrows the missing claw.

Tip: For best results, be careful not to overcook stonecrabs.

Shellfish Stew
Serves 4

16 mussels
16 littleneck clams
¼ cup (60 ml) cornmeal
16 large shrimp (16-20 count)
1 cup (250 ml) diced pancetta (or substitute high-quality bacon)
1 tablespoon (15 ml) plus ½ cup (125 ml) extra virgin olive oil, divided
¼ cup (60 ml) minced garlic
1 cup (250 ml) minced ramps (wild leeks), white part only
3 cups (750 ml) dry white wine
1½ teaspoons (7 ml) crushed red pepper flakes
8 cups (2 l) stock or broth
Sea salt and coarsely ground black pepper
½ cup (125 ml) chopped flat-leaf parsley
¼ cup (60 ml) chopped fresh oregano
¼ cup (60 ml) chopped fresh thyme
3 tablespoons (45 ml) lemon juice
1 cup (250 ml) grated Parmesan cheese
1 French baguette, sliced

Debeard the mussels and rinse in cold water. Rinse the clams and soak in cold water with the cornmeal for 1 hour. Remove the clams from the water/cornmeal mixture and rinse again. Peel and devein the shrimp.

Heat a medium stockpot or Dutch oven over medium-high heat for approximately 4 minutes. Add the pancetta to the pot and sauté until brown, about 15 minutes.

Then add 1 tablespoon (15 ml) of the olive oil to the same pan and turn the heat to high. Add the garlic and ramps and sauté for 3 minutes. Add the white wine and cook until the volume is reduced by half. Add the shellfish, shrimp, red pepper flakes, and stock. Bring to a boil and simmer for 5 to 10 minutes or until the clams are completly open and the shrimp is pink.

Adjust the seasoning with salt and pepper. Stir in the parsley, oregano, thyme, lemon juice, and remaining ½ cup (125 ml) olive oil. Discard any clams or mussels that do not open.

To serve, divide the stew among four large bowls and top with the cheese. Serve with the baguette slices.

Stonecrab Dip
Makes 2 cups

1 cup (250 ml) mayonnaise
1 cup (250 ml) crème fraîche
2 tablespoons (30 ml) dry mustard
1 teaspoon (5 ml) balsamic vinegar
1 teaspoon (5 ml) Worcestershire sauce
1 teaspoon (5 ml) hot pepper sherry
1 teaspoon (5 ml) paprika
1 tablespoon (15 ml) fresh minced parsley

Stir together the mayonnaise and crème fraîche in a mixing bowl. Whisk in the dry mustard, vinegar, Worcestershire, hot pepper sherry, paprika, and parsley. Mix until well blended and creamy.

Northern Pike en Papilotte

Serves 4

2 carrots, julienned
2 parsnips, peeled and julienned
1 rutabaga, peeled and julienned
2 shallots, minced
1 medium onion, sliced thin
1 whole leek, trimmed and julienned
½ cup (120 ml) unsalted butter, divided
1 cup (250 ml) heavy cream
6 tablespoons (100 ml) dry sherry
4 (8-ounce/225 g) northern pike fillets
Salt and pepper
8 ounces (220 g) wild mushrooms, sliced (shiitake
or Portobello mushrooms may be substituted)

In a large saucepan, combine the carrots, parsnips, rutabaga, shallots, onion, leek, and ¼ cup (60 ml) of the butter over medium-low heat. Simmer the vegetables until tender. Remove the vegetables from the saucepan with a slotted spoon and reserve the liquids.

Add the cream and sherry to the reserved liquid and simmer over low heat to reduce until the mixture thickens slightly. Keep warm.

Skin the fillets and remove any bones that remain. Season with salt and pepper.

Preheat the oven to 375°F (190°C).

Cut four pieces of parchment paper, each measuring 18x24 inches (46x61 cm). Fold each piece in half. Using kitchen shears, cut each paper to form a heart shape when unfolded.

Melt the remaining ¼ cup (60 ml) butter. Brush both sides of the parchment paper with the butter and place one fillet in the center of each paper. Layer the vegetables, reduced sauce, and sliced mushrooms on top of the fillets. Fold over the paper to encase the fillet, beginning at the widest end of the envelope and pleating the paper to fold around the edge of the envelope, creating a firm seal. When you reach the end of the envelope, close tightly with a twisting fold and tuck under the envelope. Repeat with other fillets. Place the packages on a baking sheet in a single layer.

Bake for 15 to 20 minutes, until the paper puffs up and turns golden brown. The envelope should be opened table side to fully appreciate the wonderful aroma of this presentation.

Low Country Shrimp Boil

Serves 10 to 12

Melted butter and seafood sauce complement the meal.

3 smoked venison sausage or kielbasa, cut into 1-inch (2.5 cm) pieces
8 medium potatoes, cut into 2-inch (5 cm) pieces
3 onions, cut into 2-inch (5 cm) pieces
3 ribs celery, cut into 2-inch (5 cm) pieces
¼ cup (60 ml) Old Bay seasoning, or to taste
10 to 12 ears corn, halved
5 pounds (2.25 kg) shrimp
3 to 4 pounds (1.4 to 1.8 kg) crab legs (optional)

Bring a large pot half-filled with water to a boil over medium-high heat. Add the sausage, potatoes, onions, celery, and Old Bay seasoning and boil for 20 minutes, until the potatoes are tender. Add the corn, shrimp, and crab legs, if using. Simmer for 3 to 4 minutes, until the shrimp turn pink. Drain and serve immediately on large platters.

Wild Striped Bass Misoyaki

Serves 4

I love firm saltwater fish broiled with a miso marinade. The quality of miso, a very salty fermented bean paste, varies considerably. This recipe calls for white miso, a slightly sweeter, milder version than red miso.

MARINADE:
1 cup (250 ml) white miso
½ cup (100 g/125 ml) sugar
½ cup (125 ml) sake
2 teaspoons (10 ml) grated fresh peeled ginger
Juice of ½ lemon

1½ pounds (675 g) striped bass fillets

To make the marinade, combine the miso, sugar, sake, ginger, and lemon juice in a bowl and blend together with an immersion blender. Place the fillets on a broiling pan and pour half of the marinade over fillets, reserving the remainder for basting the fish. Marinate for 15 minutes.

Meanwhile, preheat the broiler to high and set the rack as close as possible to the flame. Broil the fish, watching carefully for the sauce to begin bubbling and browning, about 5 minutes. Remove from the heat and baste fish with the remainder of marinade. Continue to broil—sugar will burn easily, so adjust the rack if necessary—until fish is cooked through and firm to touch.

Serve immediately.

Bass

What comes to mind when you think of blackened fish? Orange flames pawing out from underneath a cast-iron pan, the sizzling and smoke, and maybe some sultry Cajun music on a night too hot to sleep? They just go together!

Savory spices joined with a special frying technique was the key to fame for New Orleans chef, Paul Prudhomme, creator of the original blackened redfish. The feisty, fiery nature of this preparation set a precedent in fish cookery. Its popularity swept the nation, and has been popular ever since.

The bass is a readily available freshwater fish found throughout North America. It is a great alternative to redfish and holds up well to blackening, given its moderately firm texture.

Sweets and Desserts

Fields, forests, and meadows are treasure troves of wild fruits, nuts, perfumed flowers, honeybees at work, and maple syrup. Whether you're an experienced wild forager or a novice, the act of harvesting these edible gems brings sparkling rewards to the palate.

Desserts that come straight from nature have that earthiness, piquancy, and voluptuous juiciness that satisfy our taste buds as no other sweet can.

Hazelnuts

The hazelnut is often called filbert and grows wild throughout North America.

Make sure you have a pair of gloves for gathering these nuts, as the silvery husks are prickly on the fingers.

Hazelnuts can be cracked from the shell and eaten fresh, or the kernels can be extracted from the shells and roasted in a moderate oven for about 8 minutes or until slightly brown. This gives them a sweeter, nuttier taste. For recipes, chop by hand with a good knife or run small amounts through a coffee grinder.

Shelled nuts should be stored in an airtight container. Unshelled nuts can be stored in a cool, dry place for years.

If you're a forager who likes to stash away a few treats for winter, then you'll love the addition of these tasty little nuts to your pantry.

Maple Hazelnut Galette
Serves 6

FILLING:
1 cup (250 ml) granulated maple sugar
1 cup (250 ml) pure maple syrup
1 cup (250 ml) dry, unseasoned white bread crumbs
½ cup (125 ml) chopped hazelnuts, roasted and skinned (optional)
½ cup (125 ml) half-and-half
2 large eggs
¼ teaspoon (1 ml) salt
1 tablespoon (15 ml) wine vinegar

PASTRY AND TOPPING:
Dough for 1½ pies
½ cup (125 ml) hazelnuts, roasted, skinned, halved
1 egg white, loosely beaten with 1 tablespoon (15 ml) water
1 tablespoon (15 ml) maple sugar
1 tablespoon (15 ml) (30 ml) frangelico, hazelnut liqueur (optional)

Preheat oven to 350°F (180°C). In a mixing bowl, combine filling ingredients and mix well. Turn into a buttered 3-quart (3 l) casserole and bake uncovered for 45 minutes.

Allow filling to cool and stiffen before assembling galette. Store in refrigerator if not assembling within 1 hour (keeps up to 5 days). If necessary to soften for handling, warm filling for 1 or 2 minutes in microwave until it has the consistency of thick jam.

To assemble and bake, increase oven temperature to 400°F (200°C). On floured surface, roll dough, ⅛ inch (3 mm) thick, into 12-inch (30.5 cm) rounds or 9x13-inch (23x33 cm) rectangles. For individual galettes, cut into six 5-inch (12.7 cm) rounds.

Place pastry on buttered baking sheet. Spoon filling onto pastry and spread, leaving 1½-inch (3.8 cm) unfilled margin. Fold, pleat, and press edge around filling. Decorate with nut halves. Lightly brush entire surface with egg wash, sprinkle with maple sugar. Bake 20 minutes.

Serve warm or room temperature with ice cream or whipped cream flavored with frangelico.

Glazed Hickory-Nut Clusters
Yields about 1 ½ cups (375 ml)

3 tablespoons (50 ml) honey
¼ teaspoon (1 ml) sugar
¼ teaspoon (1 ml) salt
¼ teaspoon (1 ml) apple pie spice, curry powder or blackening spices
1½ cups (375 ml) broken hickory nutmeats (or butternuts, black walnuts, pecans)

Preheat oven to 425°F (220°C). Line full-sized baking sheet with foil. Spray foil generously with nonstick spray. In a mixing bowl, stir together the honey, sugar, salt, and spices. Add nutmeats; stir gently to coat.

Spread nuts evenly on foil-lined baking sheet. Bake 5 to 8 minutes, until golden brown, stirring every few minutes. (Remove from oven before nuts are as dark as you'd like, because they will continue to darken after you remove them from the oven.)

Cool completely before storing in an airtight container. Use as a snack, or to top tossed salads or ice cream.

Blueberry Cobbler
Serves 12

½ cup (125 ml) sugar
1 tablespoon (15 ml) cornstarch
¼ teaspoon (1 ml) cinnamon
4 cups (1 l) blueberries
1 teaspoon (15 ml) lemon juice
3 tablespoons (50 ml) butter-flavored shortening
1 tablespoon (15 ml) sugar
1½ teaspoons (7 ml) baking powder
½ teaspoon (2 ml) salt
1 cup (250 ml) flour
½ cup (125 ml) milk

Preheat oven to 350°F (180°C). Mix sugar, cornstarch and cinnamon in saucepan over medium heat. Stir in berries and lemon juice. Cook, stirring constantly, until mixture thickens and boils. Boil and stir 1 minute.

Pour into ungreased 2 quart (2 l) casserole; keep berry mixture hot in oven. Cut shortening, sugar, baking powder and salt into flour until crumbly. Stir in milk.

Drop dough by 6 spoonfuls onto hot berry mixture. Bake for 25 minutes or until berries are bubbling on the edges of the pan and the topping is golden brown. Serve warm with whipped cream.

Maple Sugar Candy
Yields about 2 pounds (1 kg)

Rubber candy molds work best; plastic, metal or wooden molds lightly greased work also. Shallow aluminum pans are options too. Adding a bit of milk, cream, or butter keeps the foam down and the syrup from boiling over.

4 cups (1 l) pure maple syrup
½ teaspoon (2 ml) milk, cream or butter

Preheat the maple syrup and milk, cream, or butter in a large pot or pan over medium-high heat to 250°F (120°C), about 10 to 15 minutes. Take off the heat to let the bubbles calm for about 1 minute.

Gently stir the hot, thickened syrup with a wooden spoon until you just begin to see granules/crystals forming, about 1 to 2 minutes. (This is tricky; if you stir too long the thickened syrup will "set up" or harden in the pan. If you don't stir long enough, the sugar may harden in the molds.)

Working quickly, pour the syrup into molds. While the sugar is still soft, use straightedge spatula to pack syrup into the molds and smooth the surface. Allow 30 minutes to cool. When they are hard, pop them out of the molds and set them on a rack to fully cool. Store in an airtight container.

Serve as an after-dinner sweet treat, or anytime!

Cranberry Dessert
Serves 9

2 cups (500 ml) flour
1 cup (250 ml) sugar
⅔ cup (150 ml) milk
2½ (12 ml) teaspoons baking powder
3 tablespoons (50 ml) oil
1 egg
2 cups (500 ml) cranberries

TOPPING:
½ cup (125 ml) butter
1 cup (250 ml) sugar
¾ cup (175 ml) half-and-half

Preheat oven to 350°F (180°C). Mix flour, sugar, milk, baking powder, oil, and egg together in bowl. Mix in cranberries.

Place mixture in a greased 9x9-inch (2 l) pan and bake for 40 minutes or until a toothpick inserted comes out clean. If you use a bread loaf pan, bake for 50 minutes.

For the topping, in a medium saucepan heat butter, sugar and half-and-half; stirring constantly, bringing to a boil over medium-high heat. Continue stirring and boil 5 minutes until thickened.

Drizzle over warm slices of cranberry dessert and serve.

Pears in Rosewater
Serves 4

This light dessert bridges the romance of late summer to early fall with the musky, exotic overtones of honey, roses, and freshly ground cardamom.

Serve it with deceptively heavy yogurt cheese or deceptively light pistachio cream panna cotta.

2 large firm pears or several smaller ones, peeled, cored and cut into wedges
1 cup (240 g/250 ml) sugar
1 cup (250 ml) white wine
12 cardamom pods, husks removed, black seeds pulverized
1 tablespoon (15 ml) rosewater

Combine sugar, wine, cardamom, and rosewater in a 4-quart (4 l) saucepan. Add pear wedges. Bring to a boil over medium-high heat. Reduce heat to simmer and cook for 30 minutes uncovered.

Spread yogurt cheese (drain yogurt overnight in refrigerator suspended in a muslin bag) on a dessert plate and sprinkle with chopped unsalted pistachios; place pears and syrup on top.

Mocha Crème Brulée

Serves 10

MOCHA CRÈME BRULÉE:
8 egg yolks
1 cup (250 ml) sugar
2 cups (500 ml) heavy whipping cream
¾ cup (175 ml) strong espresso
1 vanilla bean, cut lengthwise
Chocolate for grating, dark, semisweet or bittersweet

HAZELNUT AND SUGAR CRACKLE:
½ cup (125 ml) shelled, skinned and toasted hazelnuts
½ cup (125 ml) sugar

For mocha crème brulée, stir egg yolks and sugar in a mixing bowl. In a saucepan, heat cream, brewed espresso and vanilla bean; don't scald or boil cream mixture. Add small about of cream mixture to egg and sugar and stir vigorously.

Preheat oven to 300°F (150°C).

Continue adding cream mixture to egg/sugar mixture in small amounts until completely mixed. Remove vanilla bean.

Put mixture back on stovetop to heat and stir constantly. Test doneness by dipping the back of a spoon in mixture until it forms a film.

Pour into small, bake-proof dishes (8-ounce/225 g ramekins work well) and bake 60 to 70 minutes in a water bath, or until a digital thermometer inserted into mixture reads 180°F (82°C). Remove from oven and refrigerate until completely cool.

For crackle, grind hazelnuts and mix with sugar. Spread evenly across the crème brulée, and caramelize with propane torch: Set torch flame to about 4 inches (10 cm) long. Holding tip of flame about 1 inch (2.5 cm) above the dish, move the flame in quick strokes back and forth over the sugar mixture until it melts and turns golden brown, about 15 minutes for each serving.

Serve immediately.

Candied Wild Violets

Serves 4 (makes 36 candied violets)

Capture spring. Sprinkle it with sugar and make it stay in a little jelly jar until you need it to decorate a cake in the dead of winter. Or serve these pretty little confections atop ice cream or flan—they turn plain desserts into something beautiful.

SPECIAL EQUIPMENT:
Small paintbrush
Tweezers (beading tweezers work best)
Waxed paper

3 dozen clean, unsprayed woodland violets (white, yellow, or violet)
1 egg white blended with 1 tablespoon (15 ml) water
½ cup (125 ml) superfine granulated sugar, tinted to match flower*

With a paper towel handy, dip the paintbrush into the eggwhite-and-water mixture and dab excess off on towel.

Holding a violet with tweezers, paint a light coat of egg white outside and inside the flower. This will take some patience, because the petals tend to collapse and stick together, but with practice, you'll soon acquire the right touch.

Dip the open flower facedown into the colored sugar. Using a spoon, sprinkle the back of the flower generously with colored sugar. Lightly press to make sugar adhere better.

Set aside, placing flower facedown on wax paper to dry. Repeat the process until all flowers are completed. Allow flowers to dry completely for several days in a well-ventilated area. If not eaten immediately, store in a small jelly jar with an airtight lid.

Place on serving dish to pass.

*If using a liquid or paste food coloring (as opposed to powdered), tint sugar several days before making violets and spread out on a tray to allow time to dry thoroughly. Once dry, pulverize lumps and sift through a sieve until fine again. Picked violets will last several days in a sealed plastic bag with damp toweling placed in the refrigerator.

Raw Honey

To make honey from nectar, honey bees remove much of the moisture and add enzymes that change the composition of the nectar. We can then remove the sealed combs from the beehives to use them on our table as comb honey or extract into liquid honey.

You can substitute honey for sugar in almost any recipe. For every cup (250 ml) you substitute, reduce the amount of liquid in the recipe by 1/4 cup (60 ml). Recipes containing honey need to be beaten longer and more vigorously than sugar recipes, and when baking with honey, add 1/2 teaspoon (2 ml) baking soda for each cup (250 ml) of honey used, and lower the temperature by about 25°F (45°C). Also, batter using honey becomes crisp and browns faster than batter using honey.

Honey provides a firmer, heavier texture to your finished dish. And depending on the source of the nectar, honey flavors can range from mild and, some say, bland to quite strong and pungent.

Wild Plum Sake Sorbet
Serves 8

Sake or Japanese rice wine is used in Japanese cuisine in much the same way that grape wine is used in European cuisine; that is, to bring out alcohol-soluble flavors and to impart a richer, rounder flavor to foods. Search out the best sake affordable, bottled for drinking (not the seasoned mirin used for cooking) for use in this recipe. Honey gives the sorbet a hint of floral flavor for a silkier taste.

SORBET:
2 pounds (900 g) ripe plums, pitted and quartered (reserve one plum for garnish)
1 cup (250 ml) dry sake, divided*
3/4 cup (175 ml) sugar
2 tablespoons (25 ml) honey
Juice of 1 lemon, strained
2-quart (2 l) Ice cream maker

BAKED WONTON GINGER THINS:
1 dozen square wonton skins, cut diagonally into triangles
4 tablespoons (60 ml) melted butter
1/4 cup (60 ml) candied ginger, minced
1 tablespoon (15 ml) turbinado or raw sugar crystals

For the sorbet, 24 hours before freezing sorbet: prepare ice cream maker by freezing canister unit (if necessary for your type of ice cream maker).

Then, 8 hours before freezing sorbet: in a 3-quart (3 l) saucepan, cook plum quarters with 3/4 cup (175 ml) sake and sugar over medium heat for 10 minutes. Remove from heat and pick out and discard skins (chopsticks work well for this task).

Add honey and lemon and simmer, covered, for 5 more minutes. Remove from heat, add remaining 1/4 cup (60 ml) sake and blend with stick blender or food processor until completely smooth. Place in refrigerator until completely chilled, approximately 6 hours.

Freeze in ice cream maker according to manufacturer's directions. Sorbet will be soft when finished churning. Place sorbet in a freezer container and freeze until set, approximately 2 hours.

For the ginger thins, preheat oven 350°F (180°C).

Place wonton skins on buttered baking sheet. With a pastry brush, butter skins on both sides. Sprinkle on candied ginger and sugar. Bake for 8 to 10 minutes, watching carefully to prevent overbrowning. Remove and cool on a rack.

Scoop sorbet balls into chilled sherbet glasses and garnish with fresh plum slices. Or serve with baked wonton ginger thins.

* If using sweet plum-flavored sake, reduce sugar.

Wild Berry Tart
Serves 6 to 8

DOUGH:
1¼ (300 ml) cups all-purpose flour
2 tablespoons (25 ml) sugar
½ cup (125 ml) butter, cut into cubes
3 tablespoons (50 ml) milk

FILLING:
5 tablespoons (75 ml) sugar
2 tablespoons (25 ml) flour
¼ teaspoon (1 ml) fresh lemon zest
6 ounces (170 g) raspberries
3 ounces (90 g) blueberries
2 tablespoons (25 ml) butter, melted
1 egg, beaten
½ teaspoon (2 ml) milk

For the dough, in a large bowl, mix flour and sugar. Add cubed butter and mix until coarse crumbs form. Add milk and mix until smooth. Shape into round ball and flatten.

Wrap in plastic or cover tightly and refrigerate about 1 hour, or until firm.

Roll dough ¼ inch (6 mm) thick on a floured surface, trying to keep it 12 inches (30.5 cm) round. Place dough on a parchment-lined baking pan or nonstick baking sheet.

For the filling, combine sugar, flour and lemon zest in a bowl. Gently add berries and roll to cover with flour.

Mound berries in center of dough, leaving about 1½ inches (3.8 cm) around the edge. Gently fold dough edge up to meet berries. Drizzle berries with melted butter. Mix beaten egg and milk and brush dough with egg wash.

Preheat oven to 400°F (200°C). Bake about 35 to 40 minutes. Let cook slightly out of the oven. Slice and serve on plates, perhaps with ice cream.

Floral Essence Cake with Blood Orange Coulis

Serves 4

SPECIAL EQUIPMENT:
Food processor
9x13-inch (3.5 l) pan, buttered and lined with buttered parchment overhanging both ends of pan
3-inch (7.5 cm) round biscuit cutter
Optional: pastry bag and squirt bottle

ORANGE COULIS:
1 tablespoon (15 ml) orange zest, divided
1 cup (250 ml) sugar
6 to 8 blood oranges, peeled and cut into pieces
Juice of one lemon
½ teaspoon (2 ml) orange flower water
½ teaspoon (2 ml) vanilla

CAKE:
1¼ cups (300 ml) sifted cake flour
½ teaspoon (2 ml) baking soda
¼ teaspoon (1 ml) salt
½ cup (125 ml) sugar, divided
¼ cup (60 ml) melted butter
½ teaspoon (2 ml) orange flower water
½ teaspoon (2 ml) vanilla
3 egg yolks
5 egg whites, room temperature
Pinch of cream of tartar

WHIPPED CREAM:
1 tablespoon (15 ml) sugar
1 tablespoon (15 ml) orange zest, divided
1 cup (250 ml) heavy cream

For the coulis, process orange zest and sugar until sugar is moist and orange-tinted. Remove from processor and place in small saucepan. Process oranges until puréed; strain and measure 3 cups (750 ml) of juice. Add orange and lemon juice to sugar mixture in saucepan. Bring to a boil over medium heat; simmer for about 10 to 15 minutes until reduced by one-third, and measures approximately 2 cups (500 ml) of thin syrup. Add orange flower water and vanilla and let cool. Reserve ½ cup (125 ml) for cake recipe and save the remainder to serve with the cake.

Preheat oven to 325°F (160°C). For the cake, combine all dry cake ingredients—minus 1 tablespoon (15 ml) of the sugar—in a mixing bowl and beat 1 minute. Add liquid ingredients through yolks and beat for another minute. Place egg whites in another bowl, add cream of tartar and beat until soft peaks form. Then add remaining 1 tablespoon (15 ml) of sugar and whip until stiff but not dry. Fold egg whites into batter, blending until smooth.

Pour into prepared cake pan and spread with spatula. Bake for 20 minutes and let cool for 10 minutes. Loosen edges of cake and lift from pan holding parchment ends. Cover pan with cake rack and invert. Cool completely. Cut into twelve 3-inch (7.5 cm) rounds, reserving scraps for another use.

For the whipped cream: mix sugar with ½ tablespoon (7 ml) orange zest. Whip heavy cream, adding sugar mixture when soft mounds form, beating just until stiff.

To assemble cake: Just before serving, ladle or squirt from a squirt bottle a small pool of orange coulis on a dessert plate. Place one cake round at center, ladle or squirt on a little more coulis, and place ¼ cup (60 ml) whipped cream (with a pastry bag or spoon) evenly on top. Place another round on top of the whipped cream layer and repeat application of coulis and whipped cream topping.

To serve, slice into serving pieces and sprinkle with remaining orange zest.

Berries

Meadows, fields, and forests are treasure troves of plump, little gems sparkling with juices. Berry hunting, picking, and cooking begins in early spring and continues through the summer into early fall.

It's exciting to find an abundant patch of wild berries. But they can be a challenge to pick—often elusive in thorny thickets; sometimes already gone if the wild birds and animals get to them first. Experienced foragers know when and where to hunt, and what signs to look for. With a little practice, the novice can learn quickly!

Once harvested, berries are sweet inspirations to continue hunting in the field. At home, they lend themselves to jams, jellies, syrups, pies, tarts, cobblers, sorbets, ice cream, and reduction sauces.

Among the species found in North America are blueberries, blackberries, chokecherries, cranberries, gooseberries, raspberries, frost grapes, dewberries, and pincherries.

Pumpkin Cheesecake
Serves 12

CHEESE FILLING:
1 cup (250 ml) whole milk ricotta cheese
1 cup (250 ml) goat cheese
1 cup (250 ml) cream cheese
1 tablespoon (15 ml) sugar
1½ roasted and pureed pumpkins
2 teaspoons (10 ml) vanilla
3 eggs
1 pinch of cinnamon
1 pinch of allspice
1 pinch of nutmeg

WALNUT CRUST:
1 cup (250 ml) walnuts, halves or pieces
½ cup (110 g/1 stick) butter
2 tablespoons (25 ml) granulated sugar
1 egg yolk
1 tablespoon (15 ml) flour

DRIED FRUIT COMPOTE:
½ cup (125 ml) figs
½ cup (125 ml) golden raisins
½ cup (125 ml) dark raisins
½ cup (125 ml) tart dried cherries
½ cup (125 ml) apricots
¼ cup (125 ml) honey
1 cup (250 ml) orange juice
½ cup (125 ml) wine (white, red, or any fortified wine)

For the filling, mix the three cheeses with granulated sugar and pumpkin purée until smooth. Add vanilla, eggs, and spices; mix thoroughly. Refrigerate and proceed with the crust.

For the crust, preheat oven to 300°F (150°C). Lightly toast walnuts in oven, 15 to 20 minutes stirring occasionally. Process walnuts, butter and sugar in food processor until smooth; add egg yolk and flour and process until all are incorporated.

Increase the oven temperature to 375°F (190°C). Hand press crust dough into a 9-inch (23 cm) springform pan about ½ inch (1.3 cm) thick and bake for 20 to 30 minutes.

Let cool to room temperature and pour cheesecake filling into springform pan. Bake for 40 to 50 minutes until set and toothpick comes out clean. Cool cheesecake out of oven.

For the compote, cut figs into quarters, cut apricots into slivers. Add all fruit to a saucepan and add honey, orange juice, and wine. Simmer very slowly on medium heat for about 30 minutes until fruit has plumped up and all liquid is gone.

Serve compote on top or on the side of the cheesecake.

Fresh Strawberry Pie

This refreshing pie is a cool treat on summer days and makes a colorful plate to wrap up a meal.

1 baked and cooled single pie crust
1 quart (1 l) fresh or wild strawberries, washed and hulled, divided*
1 cup (240 ml) sugar
3 tablespoons (45 ml) cornstarch
1 cup (240 ml) water
Frew drops of red food coloring
Whipped cream

Make and bake a single pie crust according to your favorite recipe. Cool thoroughly.

Chop 1 cup (240 ml) of the strawberries. Combine sugar and cornstarch in a 2-quart (2 l) double boiler. Stir in water gradually until smooth. Add chopped berries. Cook, stirring constantly, until mixture thickens and boils, 5 to 7 minutes. Stir in food coloring. Cool.

Pour three-quarters of the syrup mixture into prepared pie shell. Stand the remaining strawberries in pie shell, reserving 3 large berries (sliced) for garnish. Pour remaining syrup over standing strawberries. Chill until firm (about 3 hours). To serve top each slice with whipped cream and a slice of reserved strawberry.

Reserve the largest berries for standing in the pie shell.

Wild Mint Iced Tea
Serves 4

Mint tea seems to offer a soothing effect to those who imbibe it. Here's a natural way to make a sun-steeped version.

1 quart (1 l) water
8 stalks wild mint with leaves, rinsed thoroughly
4 tea bags

In large glass container, combine all ingredients. Seal with lid. Let steep in the sun for several hours throughout the day. Remove the mint and tea bags and serve over ice.

Baked Apples
Serves 5

5 large apples

STUFFING MIXTURE:
¼ cup (60 ml) chopped walnuts
¼ cup (60 ml) chopped raisins
¼ cup (60 ml) chopped dried apricots
¼ cup (60 ml) brown sugar
½ teaspoon (2 ml) cinnamon
2 tablespoons (60 ml) butter, cut into 5 equal pieces

¾ cup (180 ml) boiling water

Preheat the oven to 350°F (180°C).

Core apples, saving ¼ to ½ inch (6 to 12 mm) of the bottom of each core; use these to "plug" the bottom of each apple. Make a cut in the apple skin around the "equator" of the apple. Don't cut deeply into the flesh of the apple, just deep enough to cut the skin.

In a large bowl, combine ingredients for the stuffing mixture. Divide stuffing mixture among the apples, spooning into the hollow centers. Place them into a glass casserole dish.

Add boiling water. Cover and bake for 40 to 50 minutes.

Serve warm, drizzling some of the cooking juices over each apple.

Nutrition Information

If a recipe has a range of servings, the data below applies to the greater number of servings. If the recipe lists a quantity range for an ingredient, the average quantity was used to calculate the nutritional data. If alternate ingredients are listed, the analysis applies to the first ingredient.

	Calories	Fat (g)	Sodium (mg)	Protein (g)	Carbs (g)	Cholesterol (mg)
Apple Quail	427	26	438	33	14	140
Artisan Cheese Plate	358	28	715	18	10	63
Baked Parmesan Halibut	376	19	614	35	14	62
Bear Wellington Astoria	1,087	87	570	43	35	170
Best Salmon Ever	709	46	717	49	27	187
Billy's Basted Eggs	411	34	662	20	5	278
Bison Burger	710	31	494	57	47	149
Blackened Salmon	238	10	1,042	32	2	89
Blueberry Cobbler	139	4	166	2	25	1
Braised Leg of Venison	569	12	1,752	52	63	153
Braised Spinach	264	24	183	7	8	62
Brandied Goose	2,687	236	1,274	109	25	550
Breaded Perch Fillets	541	28	372	31	41	134
Breast of Grouse w/Vinegar	502	38	1,037	37	4	180
Buckwheat Blini w/Smoked Trout	113	7	271	5	8	39
Cajun Pheasant Lasagna	469	24	1,215	25	31	103
Cajun Seafood Gumbo	766	46	2,624	45	41	251
Carolina Doves	322	18	124	25	15	103
Catfish Gumbo	273	13	1,507	18	21	46
Cêpes in Cream on Polenta	275	14	1,024	9	31	31
Chard Sauté w/Blue Cheese	241	18	1,852	11	12	46
Chef Schenten's Venison & Beef Pot Pie	1,117	76	655	40	68	244
Chicken w/Wild Rice Salad	478	34	293	29	13	88
Clay-Baked Rabbit w/Mushroom Sauce	574	36	314	41	20	149

	Calories	Fat (g)	Sodium (mg)	Protein (g)	Carbs (g)	Cholesterol (mg)
Cranberry Dessert	462	19	265	5	71	61
Cranberry-Orange Bread	2,153	35	2,824	34	429	275
Creamy Artichoke-Blossom Eggs	529	33	1,134	35	26	494
Creamy Yellow Potato & Mustard Soup	472	36	1,082	6	28	130
Day Boat Grouper w/Hollandaise Sauce	1,055	93	395	37	20	400
Dove Bog	296	12	604	19	27	64
Duck w/Cranberry & Black Pepper Sauce	574	32	1,611	51	18	252
Dungeness Crab Salad	619	44	585	29	28	130
Eggplant Misoyaki	116	2	946	4	19	0
Elk Sauerbraten	385	8	595	43	35	94
Fiddleheads w/Asian Dressing	86	6	1,029	4	7	0
Floral Essence Cake	875	38	517	12	125	272
Forest Mushroom & Fennel Soup	154	10	94	5	15	16
Fresh-Ground Venison Sausage	299	23	598	22	1	101
Garden Gazpacho Soup	82	1	727	3	18	0
Glazed Hickory-Nut Clusters	226	18	96	8	12	0
Goose w/Chokecherry Sauce	735	51	235	53	11	197
Grilled Sturgeon w/Yogurt Marinade	274	10	547	34	13	112
Halibut Enchiladas	282	5	844	18	40	18
Hot Wild Rice & Crayfish Spread	96	7	205	3	6	21
Jamaican "Jerk" Bear Ribs	481	21	1,781	48	19	0
Key West Conch Chowder	572	25	792	43	44	113
Lamb Chops w/Chinese Black Rice	808	61	979	33	30	133
Leek & Cheese Tiny Tarts	225	16	156	6	15	18

	Calories	Fat (g)	Sodium (mg)	Protein (g)	Carbs (g)	Cholesterol (mg)

Low Country Shrimp Boil

699	35	1,808	52	45	309

Mâche Salad

486	44	773	9	16	30

Maple Hazelnut Galette

705	31	489	8	101	88

Maple Sugar Candy

103	0	4	0	26	0

Mocha Crème Brulée

383	26	25	4	35	235

Morels on Crostini

483	35	651	7	35	85

Northern Pike en Papilotte

772	47	168	50	39	232

Pan-Fried Walleye w/Leek Sauce

613	34	898	42	36	237

Pan-Smoked Duck

111	5	411	15	1	58

Pasta, Peas & Pesto

945	49	493	32	97	42

Pears in Rosewater

262	1	4	1	67	0

Pecorino Packets

357	27	1,155	29	6	84

Pesto Panfish Roll-Ups

235	19	178	15	2	84

Pheasant Breast Roulade

1,035	47	610	46	114	173

Pheasant Roll-Ups

677	45	1,585	63	3	203

Pheasant Wild Mushroom Cacciatore

625	31	737	62	25	174

Pizza Cinghale

233	12	493	15	16	15

Pumpkin Cheese Cake

368	21	153	11	39	111

Quail w/Currant Sauce

427	25	194	22	27	115

Rabbit Soup w/Dumplings

909	35	1,704	51	97.	130

Red-Cooked Duck

185	8	4,284	21	7	63

Red Flannel Hash w/Poached Quail Eggs

196	6	249	8	27	158

Rosemary Garlic Squash

112	0	89	2	29	0

Salmon Tower w/Morels

602	26	1,002	43	51	111

Shiitake Mushroom Strudel

342	22	521	6	28	50

Shiitake Spring Rolls

178	2	465	4	34	5

	Calories	Fat (g)	Sodium (mg)	Protein (g)	Carbs (g)	Cholesterol (mg)

Smoked Salmon Dip

34	3	71	2	0	6

Spaghetti w/Baby Artichokes & Dandelion Greens

940	58	699	21	95	1

Spaghetti w/Ramps

1,015	74	421	14	80	8

Spicy Venison Sausage w/Pancetta

270	19	870	22	2	91

Spinach Pierogi

1,273	70	1,404	35	133	320

Spring Lamb or Venison Stew

557	29	919	33	41	85

Stew of Smoked Chukar Partridge

494	24	2,297	17	57	62

Stonecrab Dip

158	17	92	1	1	21

Tempura Morels w/Walleye Stuffing

723	31	908	18	94	49

Venison Bulgolgi Pinwheels

273	4	1,440	36	21	90

Venison Chops w/Juniper Sauce

424	14	1,593	64	7	166

Venison Meatballs

91	5	158	5	7	31

Venison Medallions

590	48	960	31	10	195

Venison w/Balsamic Vinegar

381	25	329	34	5	177

Watercress Salad

48	5	9	1	1	0

Wild Asparagus Frittata

442	34	334	23	14	452

Wild Berry Tart

284	16	158	4	33	66

Wild Boar Shoulder w/Sage & Onions

267	15	249	26	6	95

Wild Leek Soup

204	10	711	4	26	31

Wild Plum Sake Sorbet

313	7	136	2	56	17

Wild Rice & Chicken-of-the-Woods Mushrooms

38	4	40	0	1	10

Wild Rice Cakes

203	16	311	3	13	45

Wild Rice Mélange

194	7	53	7	27	12

Wild Rice Pancakes w/Apples

642	34	540	12	75	143

Wild Rice Sauté

160	8	393	4	18	16

Wild Striped Bass Misoyaki

295	6	1,372	34	22	136

Contributors

Our sincere gratitude goes to all the people who contributed recipes.

Tim Anderson
Iven's on the Bay
Baxter, MN
www.ivensonthebay.com
Chard Sauté with Blue Cheese
Stew of Smoked Chukar Partridge

Matt Annand
Prairie Bay Restaurant
Baxter, MN
www.prairiebay.com
Forest Mushroom and Fennel Soup
Smoked Pheasant Autumn Roll

Don Berger
Wyoming, MN
Cranberry-Orange Bread
Double Buttermilk Pancakes with Blueberry Sauce
Pheasant Roll-Ups
Pickled Pike

Susan Binkley
St. Paul, MN
Buckwheat Bilini with Smoked Trout
Candied Wild Violets
Cêpes in Cream on Polenta with Wilted Greens
Chanterelles with Mashed New Potatoes
Clay-Baked Rabbit with Wild Mushroom Sauce
Creamy Artichoke-Blossom Eggs
Eggplant Misoyaki
Floral Essence Cake with Blood Orange Coulis
Frisée Fennel Salad
Mâche Salad
Maple Hazelnut Galette
Pan-Smoked Duck
Pears in Rosewater
Pheasant Wild Mushroom Cacciatore
Shiitake Spring Rolls
Venison Bulgolgi Pinwheels
Venison Chops in Juniper Marinade
Wild Game Rendang
Wild Plum Sake Sorbet
Wild Rice and Chicken-of-the-Woods Mushrooms
Wild Striped Bass Misoyaki

Denise Bornhausen
Minneapolis, MN
Wild Strawberry Pie

Kirk & Gene Boyer
Boyer's Adventure Outfitters
Lino Lakes, MN
Baked Parmesan Halibut
Best Salmon Ever
Halibut Enchiladas
Cajun Pheasant Lasagna

Steven Brown
Levain
Minneapolis, MN
www.restaurantlevain.com
Dungeness Crab Salad
Salmon Tower with Morels
Spinach Pierogi

Frank Calistro
New Brighton, MN
Pasta, Peas, and Pesto

Jim Casada
Rock Hill, SC
Apple Quail
Carolina Doves
Dove Bog
Low Country Shrimp Boil
Quail with Currant Sauce
Venison Meatballs

Philip Dorwart
Tryg's, An American Restaurant
Minneapolis, MN
www.trygs.com
Panko-Coated Walleye with Pickled Cattail Shoots

Mark Emery
Ocala, FL
www.wetwaders.com
Smoked Salmon Dip

Andrew Faltynek
Timberwolf Inn
Marcell, MN
www.timberwolfinn.com
Bear Wellington Astoria
Jamaican "Jerk" Bear or Wild Boar Ribs

Ken Goff
Minneapolis, MN
Chicken with Wild Rice Salad
Creamy Potato and Mustard Soup
Duck with Cranberry and Black Pepper Sauce
Grouse with Mushrooms
Hot Wild Rice and Crayfish Spread
Venison Medallions with Maple Cinnamon Butter
Venison with Balsamic Vinegar
Wild Boar Shoulder with Sage and Onions
Wild Rice Mélange
Wild Rice Pancakes with Apples

Elliott Green
Pane Vino Dolce
Minneapolis, MN
Wild Leek Soup

Gayle Grossman
Little Moran Hunt Club
Staples, MN
www.littlemoran.com
Blueberry Cobbler
Brandied Goose
Cranberry Dessert
Goose with Chokecherry Sauce

David Hahne
Café Vin
Minneapolis, MN
Mocha Crème Brulée
Pecorino Packets
Pizza Cinghale
Pumpkin Cheese Cake

Jeff Harper
Cass Lake, MN
Maple Sugar Candy
Rabbit Soup with Dumplings

John Hunt
Al Vento Italian Cucina
Minneapolis, MN
www.alventorestaurant.com
Pheasant Breast Roulade

Jim Kyndberg
Bayport Cookery
Bayport, MN
www.bayportcookery.com
Blackened Salmon
Cajun Seafood Gumbo
Tempura Morels with Walleye Stuffing

Kay and Bill Lindner
Minneapolis, MN
Pesto Panfish Roll-Ups
Duck Chestnut Rumake
Smoked Fish Dip
Billy's Basted Eggs
Morels on Crostini
Watercress Salad
Spring Refresher
Rosemary Garlic Squash
Garden Gazpacho Soup
Breaded Perch Fillets
Key West Conch Chowder
Day Boat Grouper with Sunny Citrus Hollandaise
Stone Crab Dip

Teresa Marrone
Minneapolis, MN
www.northerntrailspress.com
Fiddleheads with Asian Dressing
Glazed Hickory-Nut Clusters
Pan-Fried Walleye with Morel-Leek Sauce
Red-Cooked Duck
Sweet and Smoky Grilled Duck

Kieran Moore
Lake Shore, MN
Autumn Squash Soup
Shiitake Mushroom Strudel
Wild Rice Cakes
Wild Rice Sauté

Matt Morgan
Craftsman Restaurant
Minneapolis, MN
www.craftsmanrestaurant.com
Red Flannel Hash with Poached Quail Eggs

Betsy Nelson
Minneapolis, MN
Pickled Ramps

Scott Pampouch
The Corner Table
Minneapolis, MN
www.cornertablerestaurant.com
Farro Risotto with Pesto and Poached Eggs
Grilled Sturgeon with Yogurt Marinade
Lamb Chops with Chinese Black Rice

Jessie Peine
Minneapolis, MN
Artisan Cheese Plate
Leek and Cheese Tiny Tarts

Mike Phillips
Craftsman Restaurant
Minneapolis, MN
www.craftsmanrestaurant.com
Braised Leg of Venison
Spring Lamb or Venison Stew

Doris Roesch
Bliss Creek Outfitters
Cody, WY
www.blisscreekoutfitters.com
Elk Sauerbraten

Michael Rostance
Broders Pasta Bar
Minneapolis, MN
www.broders.com, www.historicitaly.com
Spaghetti with Baby Artichokes and Dandelion Greens
Spaghetti with Ramps

Cliff Santa
Duluth, MN
Lake Trout Chowder

Steve Schenten
Puff Patissier
Victoria, MN
Chef Schenten's Venison and Beef Pot Pie

George Snyder
McCormick & Schmick's Seafood Restaurant
Minneapolis, MN
www.mccormickandschmicks.com
Braised Spinach

Doug Sperry
Dancing Fire Restaurant
Walker, MN
www.northernlightcasino.com
Northern Pike en Papilotte

Nathan Stausser
Nathan's Pastries
Hopkins, MN
Wild Berry Tart

Keith Sutton
Alexander, AR
catfishdude@sbcglobal.net
Catfish Gumbo

Kristen Tombers
Clancey's Meats
Minneapolis, MN
Bison Burger with Blue Cheese and Cherry Chutney

Greg Westergreen
Clancey's Meats
Minneapolis, MN
Shellfish Stew
Spicy Venison Sausage with Pancetta

Ricardo Jorge Lopes de Matos Catarrinho.
Pane Vino Dolce
Minneapolis, MN
Wild Asparagus Frittatas

Index

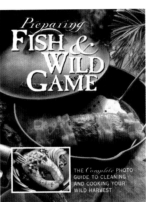

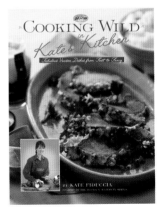